Social Studies in Action

Resources for the Classroom

Grade 1

Harcourt
SCHOOL PUBLISHERS

Orlando   Austin   New York   San Diego   Toronto   London

Visit *The Learning Site!*
www.harcourtschool.com

ISBN 0-15-344449-5

1 2 3 4 5 6 7 8 9 10 054 14 13 12 11 10 09 08 07 06 05

Contents

3   Introduction

Unit 1
4   Bag Ladies Activity
6   Drama Activity
10 Simulations and Games
12 Long-Term Project
14 Short-Term Projects
16 Writing Projects
18 Daily Geography
20 Why Character Counts
22 Economic Literacy
24 Citizenship

Unit 2
26 Bag Ladies Activity
28 Drama Activity
32 Simulations and Games
34 Long-Term Project
36 Short-Term Projects
38 Writing Projects
40 Daily Geography
42 Why Character Counts
44 Economic Literacy
46 Citizenship

Unit 3
48 Bag Ladies Activity
50 Drama Activity
54 Simulations and Games
56 Long-Term Project
58 Short-Term Projects
60 Writing Projects
62 Daily Geography
64 Why Character Counts
66 Economic Literacy
68 Citizenship

Unit 4

70 Bag Ladies Activity
72 Drama Activity
76 Simulations and Games
78 Long-Term Project
80 Short-Term Projects
82 Writing Projects
84 Daily Geography
86 Why Character Counts
88 Economic Literacy
90 Citizenship

Unit 5

92 Bag Ladies Activity
94 Drama Activity
98 Simulations and Games
100 Long-Term Project
102 Short-Term Projects
104 Writing Projects
106 Daily Geography
108 Why Character Counts
110 Economic Literacy
112 Citizenship

Unit 6

114 Bag Ladies Activity
116 Drama Activity
120 Simulations and Games
122 Long-Term Project
124 Short-Term Projects
126 Writing Projects
128 Daily Geography
130 Why Character Counts
132 Economic Literacy
134 Citizenship

136 Thinking Organizers
152 Outline Maps
158 Planning Options
170 Answer Key

Introduction

This *Social Studies In Action: Resources for the Classroom* booklet provide a variety of activities designed to help teachers facilitate and spark social studies learning in the classroom through fun hands-on projects or skill pages. Some of these activities require children to imagine they live in another time while others will prompt children to write creatively about how character, economic, or citizenship issues relate to their lives. All the included projects, activities, geography questions, drama activities, and games will help children gain a better understanding of important social studies content. The following kinds of activities are included.

Bag Ladies Activity   These activities provide children with hands-on art projects that will help them connect with social studies content in an imaginative and fun way. Only common art supplies or household items, such as brown papers bags, are required to complete the activities.

Drama Activity   These readers theatres will get children excited about social studies content by asking them to participate in an engaging storyline or tale set in the past or present.

Simulations and Games   Simulations help children gain a better understanding of social studies content by asking them to assume the role of an individual involved in a historical or contemporary situation. Games give children the chance to explore history, economics, and other social studies content in a challenging but fun and interactive manner.

Long-Term Project   These month-long projects are designed to promote cooperation as children work together to produce a presentation or artistic creation related to social studies content. Each project is divided into four sessions, and a session is completed per week.

Short-Term Projects   These projects will help children explore social studies content by singing songs, drawing pictures, making models, and so on.

Writing Projects   These writing prompts will help children use and improve their writing skills as they explore social studies content and issues.

Daily Geography   This section provides grade-appropriate questions designed to help children learn or review geography facts.

Why Character Counts   Each of these activities focuses on an important character trait. Children read about each trait, and complete a hands-on activity to reinforce understanding.

Economic Literacy   Children learn about important economic concepts and complete an activity on sound economics. Often, these activities ask children to apply economic concepts to a scenario or choice.

Citizenship   This feature is divided into three sections. Children learn about various citizenship concepts such as freedoms granted by the Bill of Rights, equality, government, and voting. Children enrich their understanding of these concepts by participating in a teacher-led debate and by completing writing activities that ask them to reflect on how citizenship concepts affect their lives.

My School Photos
Unit 1

Materials needed:

*Posterboard

*Drawing paper

*Tape

*Scissors

*Crayons, markers, or
 colored pencils

Social Studies Skills:

*School Rules

*School Workers

*Past and Present

Reading Skills:

*Main Idea and Details

*Point of View

*Compare and Contrast

Instructions:

1. Use posterboard to make the
   folder that holds the photos.
   Tape at each end to form a
   pocket. Label this pocket "My
   Photos."

2. Using drawing paper, create
   four squares inside four larger
   squares, as shown in the
   illustration. Decorate the borders.
   Then separate the four photo
   frames using a pair of scissors.

3. Create drawings in the frames
   to show workers in the school,
   school long ago and today, or
   other school topics.

Illustrations:

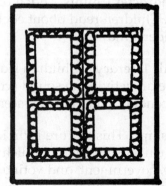

TAPE→ MY PHOTOS

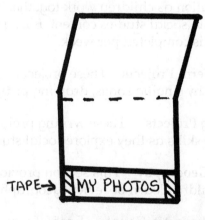

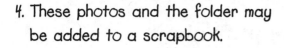

4. These photos and the folder may be added to a scrapbook.

5. You may want to cut out real photos of yourself, glue them in the photo frames, and draw illustrations around them.

Playing by the Rules

A readers theatre play about rules and laws

Cast of Characters

- Narrator
- Kendra Simpson, 7 years old
- Sound Effects
- Uncle Max, Kendra's uncle, a police officer
- Mrs. Simpson, Kendra's mother

Setting The Simpson's apartment in a large city.

Narrator: The Simpson family is making dinner. Kendra's uncle is coming to dinner.

Mrs. Simpson: Kendra, please set the table. Remember that our house rules say that we all help around the house.

Kendra: I remember. We wrote rules in our classroom, too.

Mrs. Simpson: What rules did you make?

Sound Effects: Ding-dong! (doorbell ringing)

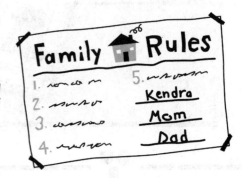

Kendra: It sounds like someone is here!

Narrator: Kendra opens the door. Uncle Max comes in. They sit in the living room with Kendra and Mrs. Simpson.

Kendra: Hi, Uncle Max!

Uncle Max: Dinner smells wonderful. I'm very hungry. I had a big day at work. The city passed a new law changing the speed limit on some streets.

Kendra: What happens if people don't follow the new law?

Uncle Max: A police officer, like me, will give them a speeding ticket.

Kendra: I guess people should not break the law.

Mrs. Simpson: Kendra's class wrote rules today.

Uncle Max: Oh, really. I'd love to hear them.

Sound effects: Ring, Ring! Ring, Ring! (the phone rings)

Mrs. Simpson: Oh, excuse me.

Narrator: Mrs. Simpson talks on the phone and then comes back.

Mrs. Simpson: That was Mr. DeLeon. He is a member of the apartment board, just like me.

Kendra: What is the apartment board?

Mrs. Simpson: It's a group of people who make safety rules for our building. We made a new rule to stop people from blocking the sidewalk with their bikes.

Uncle Max: That's not safe.

Mrs. Simpson: That's why we voted to make the new rule.

Kendra: My class voted on rules today, too.

Sound effects: Beep, Beep! Beep, Beep! (the oven timer goes off)

Mrs. Simpson: Time for dinner!

Narrator: The family sits down to eat at the dinner table.

Mrs. Simpson: Tell us about those rules now, Kendra.

Kendra: We voted on rules about how to behave. We agreed to follow the rules as best we can.

Uncle Max: What kind of rules did you make?

Kendra: We will listen to our teacher and to each other. We will work quietly, and we will be kind to each other.

> **Classroom Rules**
>
> 1. We will listen.
> 2. We will work quietly.
> 3. We will be kind.
> 4. We will share and take turns when we play.

Uncle Max: Your rules sound great. They keep people safe and happy, just like the laws in our community.

Mrs. Simpson: And like our apartment building rules.

Kendra: And like the rules in our home.

The End

Simulations and Games

Learning the Rules to Jacks Divide the class into small groups. Give each group a small bouncing ball and fifteen jacks. You could also use counters or small stones. Have the children in each group sit in a circle and place the jacks in the center. Teach them the rules for playing the game of Jacks. Explain that the game usually starts by bouncing the ball and picking up one jack at a time (onesies), then two jacks (twosies), until the player misses and is unable to get the correct number of jacks or drops the ball.

After children are comfortable playing the game, have each group decide on three new rules for play. For example, they might choose to have players pick up five jacks first, then four, then three, and so on. Or they might decide that every other turn needs to be played with your eyes closed. Have children play using their new rules. Then discuss their experience. **GAME**

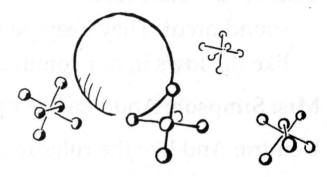

The Mayor Says... Have children play a game of *Simon Says*. Instead of having one child act as *Simon,* have the leader play the role of *Mayor.* Provide a hat labeled *Mayor* for the child playing leader to wear. Instruct the class to react to commands that begin *The Mayor Says...* but not to react to commands without this opening statement. Give all children the chance to play the mayor. **GAME**

Solving Problems   Divide the class into small groups. Give children a problem situation such as *A group of friends wants to play together at recess. Each person wants to play a different game. How will the group solve this problem?* Then invite children to role-play the scenario and come up with a solution to the problem. Have children share their performances with the rest of the class. **SIMULATION**

Acting Golden   Have children work in pairs. Invite them to act out situations that demonstrate the Golden Rule. Have them come up with at least three different examples. Give pairs an opportunity to present one of their situations to the class. **SIMULATION**

I'm Thinking of...   Play a guessing game to review the roles of leaders and helpers in the school and community. Give children a clue such as *I'm thinking of a person who leads a city.* Allow children a chance to guess the answer. Provide additional clues as needed until the leader is correctly identified. **GAME**

1 Long-Term Project

CLASS PRESENTATION: A PRESIDENTIAL PARADE

Use this project to help children understand the important job of our President and to learn more about those who have served in this role.

Week 1   Introduce
 partners   ⏰ 30 minutes

Materials: chart paper, markers, paper, pencils, poster or list of all American Presidents

Remind children of the President's role in our country. Then ask questions to get children thinking about some of our more familiar Presidents. For example, "Who was our first President?" "What do you know about Abraham Lincoln?" "Who is our country's President right now?" Explain that children will be working with a partner to find out more information about one of our country's Presidents. They will then participate in a presidential parade.

Pair each child with a partner. Direct children to a poster of American Presidents or provide pairs with a list. Read through the list of names as children follow along. Then help each pair to select a President to research. Be sure that each pair picks a different President.

Week 2   Plan
  partners   ⏰ 45 minutes

Materials: paper, pencils, resource materials, reference books, Internet Web sites

Help pairs use available resource materials to find out more information about the President they selected. Have children make a list of facts as they find them. Tell children that one fact needs to be about the President's family. Suggest they look for information about where and when the President was born.

After the children have finished their research, have pairs make a list of the three most interesting facts on a piece of paper.

Week 3 Create

  partners 30 minutes

Materials: presidential pictures or copies of pictures, magazines with presidential pictures, art materials, poster board

Provide each group with at least one picture of their President. If the President is contemporary, provide magazines from which children can cut apart images to glue on their posters. Also encourage children to draw pictures of their Presidents. Then help pairs find a quote or slogan associated with their President. Invite them to copy this onto their poster board. Have children complete their posters by adding any additional embellishments or artwork to create a visually interesting display.

After children have finished their posters, invite them to rehearse the parade. Have children begin in the hallway or the back of the classroom. Then invite each pair to march to the front, hold up their poster and tell their facts. Continue to rehearse until the children are comfortable with their roles.

Week 4 Present

 partners 30 minutes

Materials: video camera, patriotic music

Before the parade, help children invite their parents or other classrooms. Have the class present their parade. Play patriotic music, such as *Hail to the Chief* in the background as the children march and speak. After the parade, have children stand around the classroom and invite the audience members to walk around and look at the visual displays. Encourage guests to ask questions.

Tips for Combination Classrooms

 For Kindergarten students: Have children relate how some American Presidents are honored with special holidays.

 For Grade 2 students: Ask children to explain what powers the President has in the working of the government, including the President's role in making laws.

1 Short-Term Projects

Use these projects to help children learn more about rules and laws.

Rule Reminders

 partners   30 minutes

Materials: pictures of signs, poster board, markers

Show the children pictures of signs about rules such as a stop sign, a crosswalk sign, or a stoplight. Point out the words and pictures. Explain that these are visual reminders of laws in our community. Ask children if they know what each sign means and correct any misconceptions. Then make a list of school and classroom rules. Include things like *Walk in the hallways, Talk quietly,* and *Share playground equipment.* Have children work with a partner to create a reminder sign for one of the rules. Hang the signs in appropriate places around the classroom and school to remind others of the rules.

Make Ballot Boxes

 group   20 minutes

Materials: shoeboxes, construction paper, scissors, glue, markers, crayons

Have children work in small groups to create ballot boxes for classroom voting. Give each group a shoebox. Precut the lid with an opening in which the ballots can be placed. Encourage children to use color and drawings to decorate their boxes. They may also elect to add words such as: *yes, no, vote, choice.*

Comic Strip Solutions

⚉ individual 30 minutes

Materials: comic strips, blank four-block comic strip template, pencils, crayons

Show children several examples of comic strips. Explain that a comic strip tells a story in just a few boxes. Each box uses pictures and some words to tell part of the story. Have children brainstorm a list of problems that might happen in the classroom or on the playground. Examples may include sharing supplies, arguing over playground toys, or not being allowed to join a game. As a class, choose one problem. Work with children to create a four-step storyline in which the problem is solved. Write each step on the board. Then have children translate the story into a four-block comic strip. Explain that each step will be shown in one of the four blocks. Display the finished product for children to enjoy.

Classroom Chain

⚉ individual   15 minutes

Materials: strips of construction paper in two colors, markers, stapler

Give each child one strip of each color construction paper. Choose one color to represent rights and the other to represent responsibilities. Have children think about rights and responsibilities that they have at home and at school. Invite them to choose one of each and write them on the appropriate colored strip. Link and staple the strips into a chain. Hang the chain across the classroom.

Writing Projects

Use these prompts to help students think about our leaders and rules.

Elect Me

  class 30 minutes

Ask children to consider what skills it takes to be a good mayor. Encourage them to think about knowledge-based requirements as well as personality strengths such as being a good listener and caring about people and issues. Then have each child write a short persuasive speech telling why he or she would make a good mayor. Allow time for children to read their speeches in front of the class.

Saying Thank You

 class 45 minutes

Have the class brainstorm a list of things their principal does to help make their school a better place to learn. Ideas could involve school-wide actions or small gestures such as welcoming children at the door. Then write a class letter to say thank you. Rephrase their ideas to create complete sentences and model correct writing conventions. Help the class deliver the letter when it is complete.

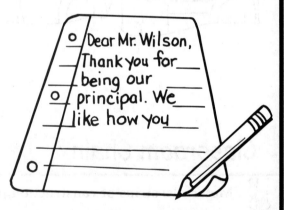

If I Were the President

 individual 15 minutes

Ask children to imagine that they were elected President. Have them write one law that they think would help to make the country a better place to live.

Bumper Sticker Advice

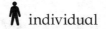 individual 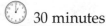 30 minutes

Review with children the fact that American citizens have the right to vote. Stress that this right gives people a chance to express what they believe. Have children make bumper stickers encouraging people to vote. Have them include a catchy phrase telling why voting is important. For example, *Voting is your right—use it!* Encourage children to decorate their bumper stickers with bold, eye-catching designs and colors.

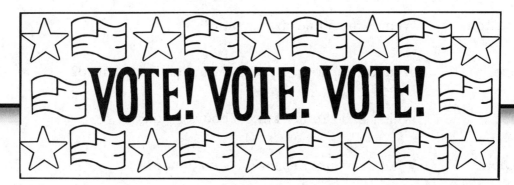

Responsibility Poem

 partners 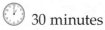 30 minutes

Have children write the word *Responsibility* vertically on a piece of paper. Then ask them to use the letters in the word to write words, phrases, or sentences that are related to the idea of being responsible. For example, next to the *R*, children could write *Rights*. Next to the *E* they might write, *everyone follows the rules*, and so on for each letter in the word. Have children share their poems and compare ideas with their classmates.

Let Me Tell You

 groups 30 minutes

Have children imagine that a new child has joined their class. Have them write a list of rules that they think this new student will need to know to do well at school. Have children include rules for different areas including the classroom, the hallways, the lunchroom, special classes, and the playground.

Daily Geography

1. **Place**	What is the name of our country?
2. **Location**	What is the name of your state?
3. **Place**	What are the largest areas of land on Earth called?
4. **Place**	Which is the largest kind of body of water?
5. **Regions**	What do mountains look like on a map?
6. **Location**	On which continent is the United States?
7. **Regions**	What are the names of the seven continents?
8. **Regions**	What are the names of the four oceans?
9. **Place**	Which kind of land has water all around it?
10. **Place**	Which kind of body of water is long and flows across the land?
11. **Human-Environment Interactions**	In which state could you see the Pacific Ocean? California Florida Illinois
12. **Movement**	Imagine that you want to travel from Arkansas to Oklahoma. In which direction will you travel?
13. **Location**	What are four states that touch the Atlantic Ocean?
14. **Location**	What are four states that touch the Pacific Ocean?
15. **Location**	What body of water touches the states between Texas and Florida?

16. Movement Which state would you pass through going in a straight line north from Missouri to Minnesota?

17. Movement Which state must you travel through to go in a straight line from Virginia to South Carolina?

18. Location Which two states touch both Canada and the Pacific Ocean?

19. Location Which state touches Canada, the Atlantic Ocean, and only one other state?

20. Location Which state touches both Mexico and the Gulf of Mexico?

21. Location Which four states touch Mexico?

22. Place Which states are larger than California?

23. Place Which state is smaller than Delaware?

24. Regions Which of these states is in the southern part of the United States?
Montana
Arkansas
Maine

25. Regions Which of these states is in the northern part of the United States?
Michigan
Florida
Arizona

26. Regions Which of these states is in the western part of the United States?
Illinois
Kentucky
Oregon

27. Place What is a large, dry area of land called?

28. Human-Environment Interactions In which state could you see the Gulf of Mexico?
Wisconsin
Alabama
South Carolina

29. Movement Which direction would you travel going from Canada to the lower part of United States?

30. Movement Which direction would you travel going from Mexico to the United States?

Why Character Counts

Trustworthiness

Being trustworthy means that people can count on you. You show you are trustworthy by keeping your promises and by being honest. Other people will know you are trustworthy when you always tell the truth.

We depend on our leaders to be trustworthy. We trust them to make good decisions.

✓**Trustworthiness**
· **Respect**
· **Responsibility**
· **Fairness**
· **Caring**
· **Patriotism**

In Your Own Words:

Why can you depend on someone who is trustworthy?

_____

_____

Name _____

Character Activity

Think about things that people trust you to do. Use the lines below to make a list. Draw a picture of yourself doing one activity from the list. Finish the sentence about your picture at the bottom of the page.

1. _____

2. _____

3. _____

I am trustworthy when I _____

_____

_____

1 Economic Literacy

Goods and Services

Look around your classroom. What things do you see? Pencils, paper, glue, chalk, and books are all goods. A good is something that can be bought and sold.

Think about what your teacher taught you today. Your teacher is giving a service by helping you learn. A service is something a person does for someone else.

There are services in your community, too. The person who drives the school bus gives a service.

Name _____

Try It

Read the list. Circle if each thing is a *good* or a *service*.

1. apple Good   Service

2. car wash  Good   Service

3. basketball Good   Service

4. backpack Good   Service

5. haircut Good   Service

6. teeth cleaning Good   Service

7. pants Good   Service

8. mail delivery Good   Service

9. teddy bear Good   Service

10. taxi ride  Good   Service

Citizenship

Read About It In the United States, citizens over 18 years old have the right to vote. Voting is a way we make choices about what we like best. Citizens vote for our President, governors, mayors, and other leaders. These leaders make our laws. When we vote for leaders we also make choices about laws.

1. Who has the right to vote in the United States?

_____

_____

2. How do we make choices about our laws?

_____

_____

Talk About It What would it be like if Americans could not choose their leaders?

Name _____

> **Write About It** Voting means making choices. If you were choosing a President, what would you want that person to be like? How would you want them to act? Include at least three examples in your answer.

_____

_____

_____

_____

_____

_____

_____

_____

_____

Prediction Postcards
Unit 2

Materials needed:

*White construction paper or index cards

*Crayons, markers, or colored pencils

*Scissors

Social Studies Skills:

*Maps and Map Keys

*Visiting a New Place

*Retelling Directions

Reading Skills:

*Predicting

*Main Idea and Details

*Sequence

Instructions:

1. Cut out postcard-size squares of paper, or use index cards. Decide on a place to write about.

2. On the blank side of the postcard, draw a picture of the chosen place. Outline the drawing with markers and color it in with colored pencils or crayons.

Illustrations:

3. On the back of the postcard, write a short letter to a friend or relative telling about the place. In your letter, ask him or her to predict what the weather will be like, where you will go next, or what will happen in that place.

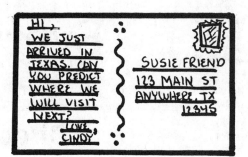

4. Students can put their postcards in a "baggy book" (a book made of pint-sized baggies) or give them to the friend or relative.

Maps, Maps, Everywhere!

Director's Notes

This readers theatre can be performed as a choral reading by dividing children into four groups, or children can be assigned specific parts if the reading is to be done by individuals.

Reader 1: It's time to go. Do you know the way?

Reader 2: No, but we have a map.

Reader 3: A map?

Reader 4: A map!

Reader 1: What will it show?

Reader 2: The map will show where to go.

Reader 1: I'm in my house and need to find the way around my town.

Reader 2: A community map is what you need.

Reader 4: Look at the map at the bottom of this page.

Reader 3: There are pictures and lines.

Reader 1: How do I know what they all mean?

Reader 2: You can use the map legend.

Reader 4: The legend tells you what all the pictures mean.

Reader 1: Oh! I see.

Reader 2: See the streets and the parks.

Reader 4: You can even find your school.

Reader 3: Yes. I see the school.

Reader 1: There is a house, too.

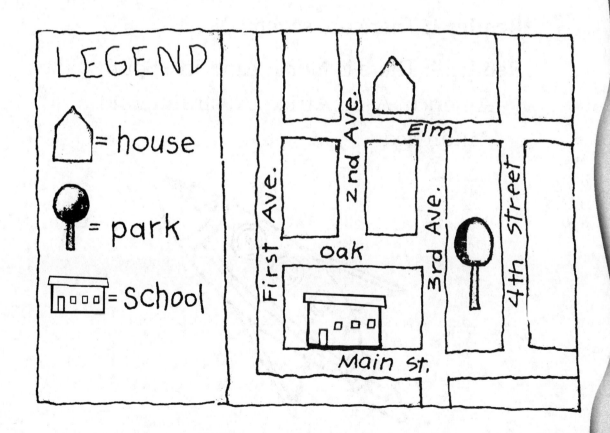

Reader 2: Wait a minute!

Reader 3: We want to see on which continent we live.

Reader 1: Do they make a map that big?

Reader 2: You bet they do. Look on this page.

Reader 4: The map shows North America.

Reader 1: Is the United States part of North America?

Reader 3: You bet it is!

Reader 2: How many continents are there?

Reader 1: There are seven.

Reader 4: There is North America, South America, Asia, Africa, Australia, and Antarctica.

Reader 2: Is there a map that shows all the continents?

Reader 3: You can see them on a map of Earth.

Reader 2: What do you think Earth looks like from out in space?

Reader 1: It is round.

Reader 3: Why are maps flat then?

Reader 2: Do they make a round map?

Reader 4: They make a round globe.

Reader 3: It shows the whole Earth as if you were looking from space!

Reader 4: You can find where you live on a globe.

Reader 1: Can I find the United States?

Reader 2: Yes. Globes show the same places as maps.

Reader 1: I think I'm beginning to see.

Reader 3: Maps and globes both show places.

Reader 1: They help show us where we live.

The End

Simulations and Games

School Tour   Pair each child with a partner. Give each pair a map of the school. Have children take turns pretending to be a visitor and the principal. Have the "visitor" ask for directions to a location in the school such as, *How do I find the gym?* Invite the "principal" to explain the route from the front door of the school to the requested location using the map and including direction like *right, left, next to, behind, around.* Encourage children to take turns playing both roles and finding several locations. **SIMULATION**

State Match   Make a set of cards showing the outline of states. For each state outline, make a corresponding card with that state's name. Have children take turns matching the outlines to the correct state name. Extend the activity by inviting children to play a memory game with the cards. **GAME**

Workers in the Neighborhood   Provide children with costumes and props appropriate for role-playing workers in a neighborhood. Have groups of children explore the costumes and pretend to be different workers. Invite them to interact with each other as if they were meeting on the street or in a neighborhood shop. **SIMULATION**

Regions Board Game

Give groups a simple template for a board game. Have them divide the board into four sections. Then ask them to label each section with one of these regions: *Coast; Mountains; Desert; Plains.* Briefly review the physical environment and weather conditions of each region. Then have children think of words and phrases that would describe the regions. Write their ideas on the board.

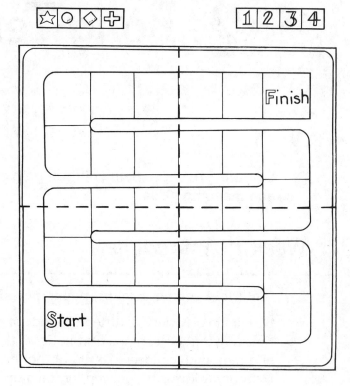

Using the children's ideas, model some descriptive statements that could be written in the game board boxes. For example, a box in the desert might read *The weather is dry. You need a drink. Go back 2 spaces.* A box in the coastal region might read: *You surf a big wave. Move ahead 3 spaces.*

Have each group make one complete game board. Then provide them with dice, and counters for pieces. Give groups time to play their games. **GAME**

Sorting Challenge

Create a three-column chart on a large piece of paper. Label the columns: *transportation, shelter,* and *food.* On index cards, glue pictures showing examples of each category. Include some word cards with examples, as well. Have children work with a partner. As one child sorts the cards into their appropriate categories, have their partner time them using a stopwatch. Invite each child to play the game at least twice, trying to beat their best time. **GAME**

UNIT 2 Long-Term Project

NEIGHBORHOOD MAP

Use this project to help children gain a greater understanding of maps and mapping skills.

Week 1 Introduce

 groups 30 minutes

Materials: compass, maps, paper, pencils

Distribute a variety of different kinds of maps. Have children spend some time looking at the maps and noticing details. Then review the components of a map with children. Point out that maps show where things are in a given location. Address the concept of the map legend. Have children find different examples of legends on the maps they have. Remind children that a legend helps you understand the symbols on the map.

Tell children that they will be creating a map of the neighborhood around their school. Spend some time discussing any special areas or locations near the school that children can recall from memory. Tell children that they will be including these and other features on their maps.

Week 2 Walk and Record

 groups 60 minutes

Materials: clipboards, pencils

Distribute materials to children. Take children on a walk in the neighborhood surrounding their school. If possible, plan on mapping a two to three block area around the school. As you walk, have children make simple sketches of places they see. They should note the names of streets, count the number of houses in a given location, note names of parks, ponds, rivers, and so on. Upon returning from the walk, conduct a discussion to review what was observed.

Week 3 Make the Map 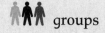 groups 60 minutes

Materials: local map, information recorded from walk, butcher paper, pencils, markers

Review the information recorded on the walk. Discuss with children what items they saw that should be included on their map. Help them to design a key to show features such as houses, parks, stores, and other objects or locations. Assign a small group of children to make the key in one corner of the map. Then lay out a large piece of butcher paper. Make a compass rose on the map. Then in the center of the paper, draw or place the symbol for the school. Next, assist children in adding the major streets around the school in the proper locations. You may wish to refer to a local map for reference. Once the streets are in place, assign small groups to work on specific areas around the school.

Week 4 Display groups 45 minutes

Materials: crayons, markers

Have children finish any areas of the map that need completion. Then have them add color and design to their map. Remind children that the map will also need a title. Display the finished product in a prominent location to allow viewing by other classes.

Tips for Combination Classrooms

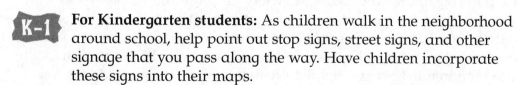

K-1 **For Kindergarten students:** As children walk in the neighborhood around school, help point out stop signs, street signs, and other signage that you pass along the way. Have children incorporate these signs into their maps.

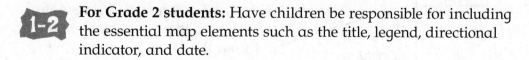

1-2 **For Grade 2 students:** Have children be responsible for including the essential map elements such as the title, legend, directional indicator, and date.

2 Short-Term Projects

Use these projects to help children explore the physical environment around them.

School Map Key

 individual   🕐 30 minutes

Materials: copies of school map, paper, pencils, crayons, markers

Give each child a map of the school. Read through it with them to identify the locations shown. Then discuss ways children might use symbols to represent the different places in the school building. For example, the art room might be shown as a box of crayons, or the gym might be represented with a ball and bat. Have children create a map legend for the school map. Encourage them to choose at least five different locations to represent with symbols. Display the legends and maps around the room.

Design a Classroom

👥 partners   🕐 30 minutes

Materials: blank classroom layout, stencils, pencils, crayons, markers

Give pairs of children a drawing showing the outline of the classroom with windows and doors marked, but without desks or furniture shown. Tell children that they are responsible for designing the arrangement of their classroom. Require that they include enough desks or tables to accommodate all the children in the class, but require nothing else. Invite children to use the stencils, or their own drawings to show how they would design and arrange their classroom. Encourage them to think about the things that are necessary to learn and the things they would like to see included. Have children create a legend for their classroom design to show features they include.

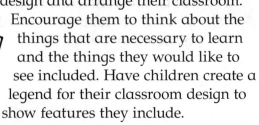

A Safe House

Materials: a traditional version of *The Three Little Pigs*, copy of *The Three Little Javelinas*, recycled containers, art supplies

Read a traditional version of *The Three Little Pigs*. Discuss with children the materials used by the different pigs and how well it was suited for the environment. Then read *The Three Little Javelinas*, an alternate version of the story set in the Sonoran Desert. Compare the materials used by the javelinas and how those materials were readily available in their environment. Point out the similarities in the two stories, especially how the first two pigs in each story designed homes that did not stand given their circumstances. Provide children with art supplies and recycled containers. Invite them to work in groups to create a house in which "fairy tale pigs" in their community could safely live. Have them consider the weather conditions and make allowances for problems with any pesky wolves or coyotes. Invite groups to explain their design to the class and describe any special or unusual features.

What I Wear

individual   30 minutes

Materials: copies of student photos, paper, crayons, markers

Discuss seasonal weather conditions and how they affect our choice of clothing on a given day. Provide children with four copies of their own photograph. Have them cut out the head portion of their picture. Then have them fold a piece of drawing paper into quarters. Assist them in labeling each of the sections on the paper with one of the four seasons: *Winter, Spring, Summer, Fall*. Then have children glue the heads from their pictures to each quadrant.

Invite them to draw the rest of their bodies dressed in clothing appropriate for the season. Children may also add other details to their pictures such as background scenery or recreational items.

2 Writing Projects

Have children complete these writing projects to gain a better understanding of the human and physical characteristics of places.

Postcard to Myself

 individual   🕐 30 minutes

Show children examples of postcards from various locations. Point out that the picture on a postcard usually shows something special about a place. Have children make a postcard for their town. Have them highlight a special building, landform, or water feature. Then on the back of the postcard, have them write a short message to themselves. Complete the activity with children writing their home address correctly on the card.

Tim Willis
IIII Blue Road
Anywhere,
CA 00000

Where Would You Live?

 individual   🕐 30 minutes

Show children examples of many kinds of homes. Include apartments, houses, farms, ranches, boathouses, and others. Have children look at the examples and then answer the following prompt: *In which house would you choose to live? Why?* Give children an opportunity to share their responses with the class.

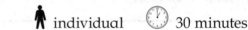

How Things Change

 group   40 minutes

Have children discuss things that change from season to season such as temperature, leaves on the trees, length of days, etc. Make a list of their responses. Then as a class, choose two seasons and write a descriptive paragraph telling of the changes that occur. Guide children to elaborate on the details in their list and add descriptive words, including sensory details.

Transportation Book

 individual   30 minutes

Have children think about places they go and the kinds of transportation they use to get there. Give each child four pieces of drawing paper. Have them use the following sentence frame to write one sentence about transportation on the bottom of each page: *I will travel to* _____ *in/on a(n)* _____ . Then have children illustrate each page to reflect what they wrote in their sentence. Have children create a cover, and bind the pages into a book.

From Here to There

 individual   30 minutes

Have children think about their favorite room at home. Then have them write directions telling how to go from the front door of their home to this favorite room. Remind them of directional words they might use. Invite children to also draw a map to accompany their written directions.

Map Riddles

partners   30 minutes

Have partners discuss the kinds of maps they know about or have used, such as a road map, a map of a building, a map showing bus routes, or a map of a park. Then have the children work together to write a riddle about one of the kinds of maps. Have them record their riddle on an index card and write the answer on the back. Use the riddles to play a game with the whole class.

2 Daily Geography

1. **Place**	What is Earth?
2. **Place**	What is a globe?
3. **Place**	What is a map?
4. **Place**	What does the title on a map tell you?
5. **Place**	What do you call the pictures on a map that stand for real things?
6. **Place**	What is the list of symbols on a map called?
7. **Location**	What are the four main directions?
8. **Location**	Which place is the farthest north you can go on Earth?
9. **Location**	Which place is the farthest south you can go on Earth?
10. **Movement**	In which direction would you travel going from the North Pole to the South Pole?
11. **Human-Environment Interactions**	Which kind of land would be the best place to have a farm? Mountain Hill Plain
12. **Location**	Which are the four largest bodies of water that touch the United States?
13. **Location**	Which large body of water does the United States touch to the east?
14. **Location**	Which large body of water does the United States touch to the west?
15. **Place**	Which one of the 50 states has water on all sides of it?

16. Movement Imagine that you and your family will travel from Colorado to Missouri. In which direction will you travel?

17. Movement Imagine that you and your family will travel from Indiana to Nebraska. In which direction will you travel?

18. Movement Imagine that you and your family will travel from Pennsylvania to Illinois. In which direction will you travel?

19. Location Which state touches large bodies of water on the east, the west, and the south?

20. Location Which states do not touch any other states?

21. Regions In which part of the United States is West Virginia?

22. Regions In which part of the United States is Oregon?

23. Location Which part of a map shows directions?

24. Region What is the line around a state or country called?

25. Location Which of these states share a border?
Wyoming and New Mexico
Texas and New Mexico
Kansas and New Mexico

26. Location Which of these states share a border?
Delaware and Virginia
Pennsylvania and Maryland
New York and New Hampshire

27. Location Which river is the border between Ohio and Kentucky?

28. Human-Environment Interactions In which state capital would you be in a desert?
Sacramento, California
Phoenix, Arizona
Baton Rouge, Louisiana

29. Human-Environment Interactions In which of these state capitals would you be in the mountains?
Denver, Colorado
Topeka, Kansas
Lincoln, Nebraska

30. Human-Environment Interactions Near which of these cities could you see a cattle ranch?
Portland, Maine
Dallas, Texas
Honolulu, Hawaii

Why Character Counts

- · **Trustworthiness**
- · **Respect**
- ✓**Responsibility**
- · **Fairness**
- · **Caring**
- · **Patriotism**

Responsibility

Responsibility means you watch how you act.

You can be responsible for how you act. You can make sure you treat others nicely. When you make a mistake, you can make things right. You can say you are sorry and help fix things.

You can show responsibilty. One way is to clean up after yourself.

Recycle

In Your Own Words:

What is one way to show responsibility?

_____

_____

_____

Name _____

Character Activity

Think about ways you can show responsibility. Pick one idea and use the space below to make a picture. Complete the sentence at the bottom about your picture.

I am responsible when I _____

_____

2 Economic Literacy

Jobs

Communities have many workers. Some people are office workers, police officers, or grocery clerks. These workers all do jobs. A job is work a person does for money. What jobs do people in your family have?

Carla's mother is a teacher. She can work anywhere there is a school. Carla's father is a fisher. He needs to live near the water to do his job.

Name _____

Try It

Read about each worker. Use the map to tell in which towns each worker would find the job they want.

1. Sarah is a park ranger. She wants to help mountain climbers. Where should she live?_____

_____

2. Jacob is a farmer. He grows corn and raises cows. Where should he live? _____

_____

3. Marla is a marine biologist. She studies fish in the ocean. Where should she live? _____

_____

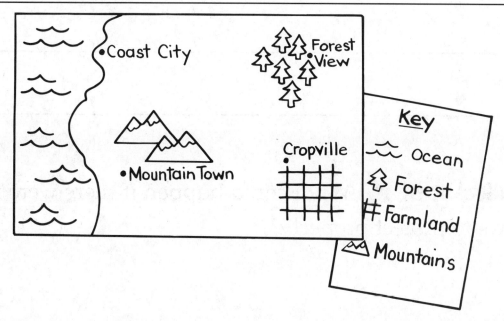

2 Citizenship

> **Read About It** People in the United States have the right to own the place where they live. Not all people choose to own their own homes. Some people rent. They pay the owner for the right to stay there.

Property is a word used to describe the place you live and your things. No one has the right to take your property unless you let them.

1. What does it mean to rent?

   _____

   _____

2. What is property?

   _____

   _____

> **Talk About It** What could happen if there were no laws to protect property?

Name _____

Write About It   Think about the place you live. Also think about things you own. Why do these things make you happy?

_____

_____

_____

_____

_____

_____

_____

_____

_____

Symbol Spinner
Unit 3

Materials needed:
*2 dessert-sized paper plates, plain white
*Brass fastener
*Crayons, markers, or colored pencils

Social Studies Skills:
*American Symbols
*Presidents
*American Landmarks

Reading Skills:
*Categorize
*Generalize
*Point of View

Instructions:

1. Mark a dot in the center of each plate.

2. Fold one plate in half. Cut a bell-shaped opening, not too close to the center dot or to the edge.

Illustrations:

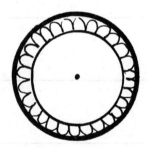

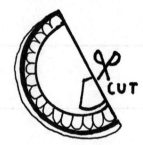

CUT

3. Open the cut paper plate and lay it on top of the uncut plate. Fasten the plates together at the dot with the brass fastener.

4. Draw and label American symbols, landmarks, or Presidents on the bottom plate in the "window" as you turn it to each new place. Or, if you prefer, create your own symbols and write captions to explain their meanings.

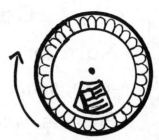

TURN AND DRAW

5. Add a title to the top plate, and turn it to share the illustrations.

Children of the Mayflower

A readers theatre about what it might have been like for children on the Mayflower.

Cast of Characters

- Narrator
- John, *young boy*
- Francis, *young boy*
- Mary, *young girl*
- Priscilla, *young girl*
- Joseph, *young boy*
- Samuel, *young boy*
- Captain Jones, *ship's captain*

Narrator: Many years ago a ship called the Mayflower sailed to North America. Many of the people on the ship were children.

Mary: I am so glad the storm is over.

Priscilla: Me, too! It is good to get some fresh air.

John: The sea is calm now. The sky is blue.

Samuel: I'm glad to see the sky. It is no fun being stuck below the deck.

Mary: John, where is your brother, Francis?

John: I think he is with my dad.

Priscilla: Does anyone know what is for dinner tonight?

Mary: We will probably have the same food as yesterday.

John: The bread is a little too hard for me.

Samuel: The sailors call the bread hardtack. I think it is supposed to be hard.

Priscilla: My mother told me that it lasts longer than normal bread because it is hard.

Mary: I hope we reach our new homes soon.

Joseph: I bet there will be lots of new foods.

John: Best of all, we can cook over a real fire.

Samuel: It will be nice to take a real bath.

Priscilla: It will also be nice to sleep without hearing the ship creak.

Narrator: Francis joins the rest of the children.

Francis: Hello, John. Hello, everyone.

John: Did you hear any news from Dad?

Francis: Yes. He was talking to Captain Jones and some of the sailors.

Samuel: I would like to be a sailor someday.

Francis: My father says it is a hard job. I want to be a farmer, like Dad.

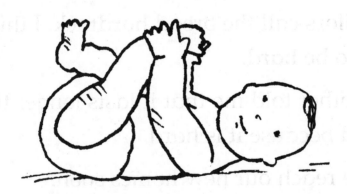

Joseph: What news did you hear?

Francis: Did you hear that a baby was born?

Mary: Was it a boy or a girl?

Francis: A boy. He is named Oceanus, after the ocean.

Joseph: Did you hear how much longer it would take to cross the ocean?

Francis: I heard Captain Jones say that our trip will be over very soon.

Narrator: The children suddenly hear someone in the distance.

Captain Jones: Land ho!

John: We're here!

All: Hurrah!

The End

Simulations and Games

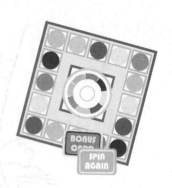

Discussing Freedom Organize the class into small groups. Review the reasons why colonists wanted to have freedom from England. Then have groups imagine that they are colonists discussing freedom. Have them talk to each other about why they should tell the king that they want to live as a free country. Remind them that the colonists thought many of the king's laws were unfair. **SIMULATION**

Date Finder Create a game board by gluing four blank calendar pages onto a piece of poster board. Label and date the calendars to reflect the months of November, December, January, and February. Then write on index cards the national holidays and other important dates that occur during these months. Include Veteran's Day, Thanksgiving, Christmas, New Year's Day, Valentine's Day, Lincoln's Birthday, President's Day, and Washington's Birthday, among others. Place the cards in a pile facedown. Then provide children with counters for keeping score. Have children work in groups. Have each group take turns drawing a card and placing it on the correct date on the calendar board. Children will get to take a counter for each correct placement. After all the cards have been placed, the child with the most counters wins. **GAME**

November

	Sun	Mon	Tue	Wed	Thu	Fri	Sat
2		1	2	3	4	5	6
9	7	8	9	10	Veteran's Day	12	13
16	14	15	16	17	18	19	20
23	21	22	23	24 Thanksgiving		26	27
30	28	29	30				

Heroic Acts   Remind children what it means to be a hero. Tell children that everyday people, even children, can be heroes. Have small groups talk about examples of heroic things that people might do, such as firefighters rescuing someone from a fire, a child calling 911 in an emergency, or a group of people collecting food to help the hungry. Have children think of an example and role-play a situation in which someone acts in a heroic way. **SIMULATION**

Symbol and Landmark Tic-Tac-Toe   Give partners a blank three-square by three-square grid. Then write and draw some American symbols and landmarks on the board, such as the bald eagle, American flag, Liberty Bell, Mount Rushmore, Washington Monument, and Capitol Building. Have partners copy one of these into each square on their grid paper. If time allows, have pairs draw a picture to represent each. Then give each child a different colored set of counters. Have partners use the grids to play tic-tac-toe games in which they identify each symbol or landmark as they choose to place their counter on top of it. **GAME**

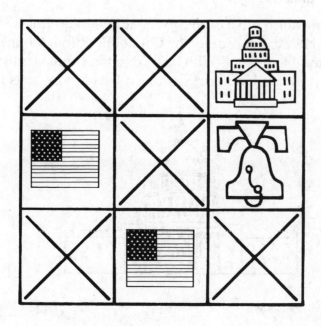

3 Long-Term Project

LANDMARK BROCHURE

Use this project to have children learn more about landmarks in the United States.

Week 1 Introduce class 45 minutes

Materials: chart paper

Review with children how landmarks are special places that remind us about people or events in our history. Point out that most landmarks have brochures or pieces of paper with information about the landmark. If possible, show children examples of some brochures. Point out that these brochures usually contain the name of the landmark, its location, history, and hours of operation, as well as information about tours and special events. Make a list of these features.

Week 2 Plan class 30 minutes

Materials: paper, pencils

Have children brainstorm a list of five to six national landmarks. These could include the White House, the Alamo, the Capitol Building, Mount Rushmore, and the Washington Monument. With help from the class, identify basic facts about each of the national landmarks. Make a list of these facts for Week 3.

Week 3   Make the Brochure  partners   60 minutes

Materials: drawing paper, colored pencils, markers, landmark photos

Divide the class into pairs. Have children create travel brochures for their landmarks. Display the list of facts about the landmarks from Week 2. Display photos of the landmarks as well. Demonstrate how to fan-fold a piece of paper into thirds to create the brochure. Remind children to include the name and a picture of the landmark on the front. Inside the children should write some words or a sentence that describes the landmark and its location. Advanced children may want to include the hours of operation and information about tour times and special events. Have the children use their imagination to come up with this information if it is not readily available.

Week 4   A Visitor's Center class   15 minutes

Materials: table or desks

Have pairs place their brochures on a table or group of desks. Label the area as the *Visitor's Center*. Invite children to explore the brochures made by their classmates.

Tips for Combination Classrooms

 For Kindergarten Students: Have children recognize how the landmarks they chose are national symbols.

 For Grade 2 Students: Have children investigate any individuals associated with the landmark they chose.

UNIT
3 Short-Term Projects

Use these projects to have children explore how national symbols relate to our country's history.

Class Flag

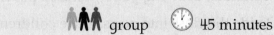 group · 45 minutes

Materials: large sized drawing paper, pencils, paint, paintbrushes

Discuss the meaning behind the symbols on the American flag. If possible, show children earlier forms of the flag and explain what the different symbols and designs meant. Then have children work in groups to design a flag to represent their class. Have them brainstorm a list of symbols that could be used. They might choose to represent the number of boys and girls, the nationalities of children  in the class, likes and dislikes of the class, class pets, or favorite activities. Remind children that colors can also show meaning. After each group has decided on a design, have them paint their flag onto a large piece of drawing paper. Display the flags along with index cards that provide brief explanations of the symbols shown.

Create a Holiday

 partners · 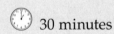 30 minutes

Materials: paper, pencils

Have children work with a partner to plan a holiday that will honor a person or event in their school or community. Invite each pair to answer the following questions about their holiday: *Who or what does your holiday honor? How will people remember or celebrate this holiday? On what day or date will the holiday be celebrated? Why?* After partners have answered these questions, have each pair take turns sharing their ideas with the class.

Class Currency

Materials: cardboard circles, paper strips, markers, scissors, glue

Show the children examples of various kinds of money. Point out that our country's money comes in two different forms: paper and coins. Explain the meaning behind some of the symbols or landmarks on money. Then have children work as a group to design their own money. Ask them to use symbols and colors to create at least one coin and one bill. Pass out cardboard circles for coins and paper for bills. Supervise children as they use scissors and glue to create the coins and bills.

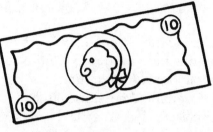

Historic Time Line

group   30 minutes

Materials: butcher paper, crayons, markers

Review with the class the historic events that lead to the founding of our country. Then create a class mural depicting a time line of the events. Assign small groups to work on each of the following: *The settlers arrive on the Mayflower. The colonies in America are ruled by England. American leaders sign the Declaration of Independence. Americans fight a war with England. American leaders write the Constitution.* Have children use pictures and words to represent their historical event. Display the completed mural in a hallway for others in the school to view.

The settlers arrive on the Mayflower.

The colonies in America are ruled by the King of England.

UNIT 3 Writing Projects

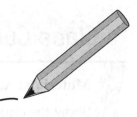

Have children complete these writing projects to gain a better understanding of our country's symbols and heroes.

Hero Story

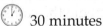 individual 30 minutes

Have children think of someone they know who is a hero. The person may be a figure in history, a famous individual alive today, or someone from their lives. Have them write a short paragraph telling why this person is special. Combine their stories into a newspaper titled *The Hero News*.

The Hero News

Holiday Book

 individual 30 minutes

As a class, choose one of the national holidays. Then make a class book telling how children and their families celebrate the event. Invite each child to complete the following sentence frame and copy it onto the bottom of a piece of drawing paper: My family celebrates (holiday) by_____. Then have children illustrate their page. Bind the pages to create the class book.

Tracking Goals

 individual 30 minutes

Talk with children about goals. Point out that it is important to keep track of the progress you make toward meeting your goals. Help children to set a goal for school. Then, each day, have children record their progress in a journal using the following sentence starters: Yesterday, I _____. Today, I _____. Tomorrow I will _____.

Classroom Pledge

 class 30 minutes

Remind children that the Pledge of Allegiance is a promise to be loyal to and support our country. Working as a class, help children to write a classroom pledge. Brainstorm behaviors that could be expected from members of the class. Then use these ideas to write the pledge. Copy the final draft onto a large piece of paper. You may opt to have the children recite the classroom pledge together.

> ### *Classroom Pledge*
>
> *I pledge to do my best to get along with other people. I will be caring. I will also work to respect other people.*

Musical Words

 individual 30 minutes

Play one or more patriotic songs for children, such as *America the Beautiful* or *The Star-Spangled Banner*. Then have children write a response to the music describing how it made them feel. You may wish to have children write words that come to mind as they listen to the music.

Settler's Diary

 individual 30 minutes

Discuss with children what it would have been like to travel to the Americas on the *Mayflower*. Point out that many children did make the long, difficult crossing. Explain that they left behind most of their belongings and had to say goodbye to friends and some family members. Talk about how this might have made them feel. Then have children imagine that they were passengers on the Mayflower. Invite them to write a diary entry sharing their feelings about the journey and their hopes for their new home.

3 Daily Geography

1. Place   What is the highest kind of land?

2. Place   What kind of land is high, but not as high as a mountain?

3. Place   What kind of land is mostly flat?

4. Place   What do you call a land and the people who live there?

5. Location   Which country does the United States touch to the south?

6. Location   Which country does the United States touch to the north?

7. Regions   How many states are there in the United States?

8. Location   Which state touches Kansas to the west?

9. Location   Which states touch Texas to the north?

10. Location   Which state touches South Dakota to the south?

11. Movement   Which states would you pass through going in a straight line north
                  from the middle of Texas to the middle of North Dakota?

12. Movement   Which states would you pass though going in a straight line west
                  from Kansas to California?

13. Place   What do you call the land between hills or mountains?

14. Place   What do you call dry land that gets little rain?

15. Human-   In which state would you find the Statue of Liberty?
    Environment
    Interactions

16. Movement   In which direction would you travel to go from the capital of Kentucky straight to the capital of Missouri?

17. Movement   In which direction would you travel to go from Lincoln, Nebraska, to Des Moines, Iowa?

18. Movement   In which direction would you travel to go from Lansing, Michigan, to Albany, New York?

19. Human-Environment Interactions   In which hilly city in California do people ride cable cars?

20. Regions   Which continent has only one country?

21. Place   Which ocean is north of North America?

22. Place   What is the largest ocean in the world?

23. Location   Which city is the capital of Washington?

24. Movement   Which ocean would a traveler cross to get most quickly from Africa to North America?

25. Location   Which ocean is east of Africa and west of Australia?

26. Location   Which ocean is east of Asia and west of North America?

27. Place   Which river is the longest in the world?

28. Place   Which country is the largest on the continent of North America?

29. Human-Environment Interactions   In which state would you find the Liberty Bell?

30. Human-Environment Interactions   In which state would you find Mount Rushmore?

Why Character Counts

Patriotism

You show patriotism when you care about your country. There are many ways to show you care. One way is to be a good citizen.

- **Trustworthiness**
- **Respect**
- **Responsibility**
- **Fairness**
- **Caring**
- ✓ **Patriotism**

Another way is to celebrate our country. You can sing songs that say our country is great. You can celebrate the Fourth of July. This special day celebrates the birth of our country.

In Your Own Words:

What is one way to show patriotism?

_____

_____

Name _____

Character Activity

Read the words to this song. Then practice singing it.

My Country, 'Tis of Thee

My country 'tis of thee,

Sweet land of liberty,

Of thee I sing.

Land where my fathers died,

Land of the Pilgrim's pride,

From ev'ry mountain-side

Let freedom ring.

Music by Henry Carey

Words by Samuel F. Smith

---

1. What is this song about? _____

_____

_____

2. How do the words to this song show patriotism?

_____

_____

3 Economic Literacy

Markets

Think of things you use each day, like soap, toothpaste, and clothing. We cannot make all the things we want. We depend on others to make goods for us.

A place where goods are bought and sold is called a market. Grocery stores and malls are markets.

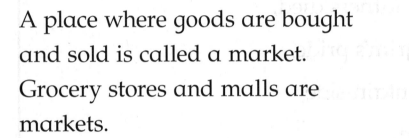

When we buy things at a market, we trade. Trading means giving one thing to get another. We trade money for goods.

Name _____

Try It

Draw a picture of one good you would buy at each of these stores. Then write the name of the good on the line under the store.

GROCERY STORE

CLOTHING STORE

_____   _____

TOY STORE

SPORTING GOODS STORE

_____   _____

3 Citizenship

Read About It Settlers came to the Americas looking for a better life. They wanted to find a place to live freely. The leaders who wrote the Declaration of Independence created a country that was free. They wrote that we are free to make choices. We are free to do the things that make us happy.

1. Why did settlers come to the Americas?

_____

_____

2. What does the Declaration of Independence say?

_____

_____

Talk About It Why do you think the Declaration of Independence is important?

Name _____

Write About It   The Constitution of the United States
is a set of rules that helps our country stay free. Which
rules in your school or classroom help you stay safe and
happy?

_____

_____

_____

_____

_____

_____

_____

_____

My Point of View
Unit 4

Materials needed:

*1-inch square of stick-on Velcro®

*Construction paper

*Drawing paper

*Colored pencils, markers, or crayons

*Glue

*Scissors

Social Studies Skills:

*Cultures

*Change

*Families

Reading Skills:

*Point of View

*Sequence

*Main Idea and Details

Instructions:

1. On the construction paper, create a setting for a topic such as "When My Grandparents Were Young, They..." or "Festivals From the Past." The setting should be drawn in pencil, outlined in markers, and colored using crayons, markers, or colored pencils.

Illustrations:

2. Using drawing paper, make a main character for the project. Dress the character and add a hairstyle or hat to show further details of the topic. You may wish to add construction-paper props to the scene.

3. Use the Velcro® to place the character where you want it in the setting.

4. Students may give oral presentations about their family history or festivals from the past using their illustrations.

Grandparents' Visit

A readers theatre about the past, the present, and change

Cast of Characters
- Narrator
- Maria
- Juan
- Mrs. Lopez
- Mr. Lopez
- Grandmother
- Grandfather
- Sound Effects

Narrator: The doorbell rings at the Lopez home.

Sound Effects: Ding-dong! (doorbell ringing)

Narrator: Mrs. Lopez opens the door. Grandmother and Grandfather come in carrying a photo album and a box.

Mrs. Lopez: It looks like you've brought something special with you.

Narrator: Maria comes into the room.

Maria: Hello, Grandma and Grandpa!

Grandfather: How are you, Maria?

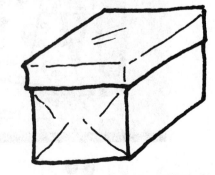

Maria: I am good. I was working on the computer. I'm writing a story for school about how life was different in the past.

Grandmother: That's wonderful! I brought something special to share with you and your brother. I think it might even help you with your homework.

Narrator: Juan comes into the room. He is holding a remote control car.

Grandfather: Wow, Juan, you have quite a toy there. What does it do?

Juan: I can drive the car with this remote control. Did you ever have a remote control car?

Grandfather: No, but I had other toys. In fact, your Grandmother and I have something to share with you and your sister.

Narrator: Everyone sits down to look at Grandmother and Grandfather's box.

Grandmother: We were cleaning our attic and found these things.

Mrs. Lopez: I remember that box. It has some of your old toys and special memories inside. You showed it to me when I was a little girl.

Grandmother: That's right. Now we thought we would share the box with Maria and Juan.

Grandfather: Let's look at the pictures in the box.

Maria: Is this a picture of you when you were my age?

Grandmother: Yes. That's my first-grade class.

Maria: Did you have a computer to do your homework?

Grandmother: No. Schools didn't have computers then. I wrote my homework in a notebook like this one. You can read stories I wrote when I was your age.

Maria: I like to write stories, too.

Juan: Grandfather, is this a picture of you? What are you holding?

Grandfather: That's me. If you look in that box, I think you will find what I was holding.

Narrator: Juan takes an old-fashioned metal car out of the box.

Juan: Wow! This car is great! The doors open, and so does the hood.

Grandfather: That was my favorite toy. It doesn't have a remote control, but I used my imagination to make it go many places.

Juan: What else did you do? Did you watch television?

Grandfather: No one had televisions when I was young. I liked to play outside.

Juan: I like playing outside, too!

Mr. Lopez: It looks like many things have changed over time.

Grandmother: Yes, but many things are still the same.

The End

UNIT 4
Simulations and Games

How We Do Jobs   Help children make a list of how technology has changed the way we do some tasks at home and at work. Include such activities as washing clothes on a washboard versus a washing machine, writing letters versus typing them on a computer, using a rotary dial on a telephone instead of punching in numbers, using a cash register with buttons instead of scanners at a store. Post the list and have children pantomime the different activities to compare and contrast the way things have changed. **SIMULATION**

Transportation Trivia   Review with children different kinds of transportation, both present and past forms. Then have each child choose one kind of transportation and write three clues about it. Collect their clues and use them to play a class trivia game. Choose one set of clues, read them aloud, and then invite children to guess the type of transportation being described. Invite the clue writer to confirm the answer. **GAME**

Life Today and Long Ago   Write the following topics on cards: school, games, transportation, and clothing. Have pairs select a card and read the topic. Invite one child to pretend to be from the past, while the other will be from the present. Invite pairs to have a conversation about the topic on their card telling how they are the same and how they are different. For example, *I go to school in a big building with many children. I go to school in a one-room schoolhouse.* Have children play through several topics taking turns role-playing each time period. **SIMULATION**

What Did I Draw? Write the names of
school tools on index cards. Include items
from both the past and the present such as an
abacus, bottle of ink, quill pen, slate, hornbook,
computer, markers, calculator, and textbook.
Place the cards facedown in a pile. Divide the
class into two teams. One team begins play by
selecting a card from the pile. After discussing
the tool quietly, have the team choose one
child to draw the item while the other team
tries to guess what it is. If the other team is
not able to guess, allow the drawing team to
provide verbal clues until the item is correctly
identified. Then have the guessing team select
a card and follow the same procedure. Continue
by having teams take turns drawing and guessing
until all cards have been selected. **GAME**

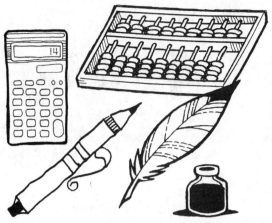

Fact and Fiction Hunt Collect a number of books,
both fiction and nonfiction. Mix up the books and place them
on a table. Pair each child with a partner and give pairs a
piece of paper and a pencil. Help children divide the paper
in half, and label one side *Fact* and the other side *Fiction*. Give
partners ten minutes to review the books and identify in
which category they belong. Have them record their findings
by writing the corresponding book titles in the appropriate
columns. **GAME**

Past or Present Have children write
Past on one piece of paper and *Present* on
a second piece. Then show them pictures,
one at a time, of people, places, and things
from the past and present times. For
each picture, have children hold up the
paper that correctly labels the time period
shown. Invite children to keep score of
their correct answers. **GAME**

UNIT 4 Long-Term Project

CHILDHOOD TIME LINE

Use this project to help children gain a better understanding of how they have changed over time.

Week 1 Introduce

 class   30 minutes

Materials: chart paper, paper, pencils

Ask children about how they have changed since the time they were babies. For example: "What did you eat when you were a baby?" "What do you eat now?" "How did you tell people what you wanted when you were a baby?" "How do you tell them now?" "What did you do for fun when you were little?" "What do you do now?" Make a list of their ideas on chart paper.

Tell children that they will be making a time line to show how they have grown and changed since the time when they were babies. Ask them to work with their parents to find four pictures of themselves. Ideally each child will bring in a baby picture, a toddler picture, a preschool picture, and a current picture. Alternatively, children could draw pictures of themselves.

Week 2 Research

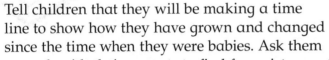 individual 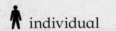 30 minutes

Materials: children's pictures, photo safe paper, magazines, newspapers, tape, index cards, pencils, markers

Assist children with mounting their photos on colored paper. Give each child four index cards. Help them to write or dictate a caption to go with each photo. If necessary, show children examples of photographs and captions from magazines and newspapers to guide them in the process. Tell them that the caption should explain what is happening in the picture in a few words or sentences.

Week 3 Create

 class 45 minutes

Materials: butcher paper, mounted photographs, tape, markers

Divide a large sheet of butcher paper into four sections. Label each section with one of the following: *Baby, Toddler, Preschool, First Grade.* Have children tape their photographs and corresponding index cards to the appropriate locations on the paper. When all the photographs are in place, invite children to use markers to decorate the area around the photos with artwork that reflects things they did, ate, wore, etc., during each time period.

Week 4 Present

 class 20 minutes

Invite parents and classmates to view the time line. Divide the class into four groups and assign each group a section. Have groups act as tour guides for their section and explain to visitors what things are shown.

Tips for Combination Classrooms

K–1 **For Kindergarten students:** Have children use time-order words to state the order in which the events are shown in their pictures occurred. For example, *First, I was a baby. Then I learned to walk. Next I learned to sing songs. Now I learn math at school.*

1–2 **For Grade 2 students:** Have children use the photographs they found to write a short family history. Invite them to gather information by interviewing their parents.

4 Short-Term Projects

Use these projects to have children explore the past and how it relates to the present and future.

One-Room Schoolhouse

 group  45 minutes

Materials: craft sticks, log-type building blocks, glue, cardboard

Have children work in groups to design and build their own model one-room schoolhouses using craft sticks or log-type building blocks. Assist groups in starting their structures and securing them to cardboard bases. When their models are complete, have groups explain their designs and compare it to their own school building.

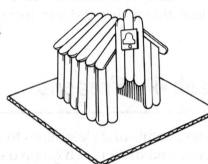

Old Fashioned Writing

group 45 minutes

Materials: berries (blueberries, strawberries, raspberries, or others), strainer, bowl, wooden spoon, small containers, feathers, scissors, paper

Set up an ink making station in one corner of the classroom. Mix various kinds of berries and place them in a strainer. Set the strainer over a bowl. Divide the class into small groups. Have groups come, one at a time, to the station. Give each child a chance to press the berries into the strainer with the back of a wooden spoon. When all children have had an opportunity to strain some juice, throw away the pulp. Add approximately 1/2 teaspoon of salt and 1/2 teaspoon of vinegar to the juice and mix it well. Then divide the juice into small cups, one for each group. This will be used as the ink. Give each group a feather with the quill cut at a slight angle, and one container of juice. Have children take turns trying to write with the feather.

School History

Materials: chart paper, pencils, index cards, artifacts

Help children to investigate the history of their school. As a class, brainstorm a list of questions about the school's history. Include the year the school was built, who it was named after, what that person did that was special, the number of principals who have led the school, the teacher who has worked there the longest, and any other ideas the children contribute.

Then invite the school librarian or the school principal to help the class find the answers to these questions. If possible, collect old photographs and any other artifacts to help tell the history of the school. When all the questions have been answered, work with children to write the facts on index cards. Then display the fact cards along with the artifacts in a window box or on a table at the front of the school.

Transportation of the Future

group · 45 minutes

Materials: drawing paper, crayons, markers

Write the following methods of transportation on the board: *Car, Train, Boat,* and *Airplane.* Review with children what these types of transportation looked like in the past and what they look like now. Then have children work with a partner to draw a picture of what they think each kind of transportation will look like in the future. Encourage them to give their vehicles a name and describe any special elements of the design. Display the drawings for others to view. Allow time for partners to tell about their designs.

UNIT 4 Writing Projects

Have children complete these writing projects to gain a better understanding of change.

How We've Grown

 class   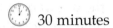 30 minutes

Lead children in a discussion of the new skills they have learned so far this year. For example, point out how much higher they can count, or how many new words they can read. As a class, write a list of ways the children have changed and grown since entering first grade. Post the list and continue to add to it throughout the year.

Interview Questions

 class   30 minutes

Remind children that they can learn about the past by talking with their grandparents or other older family members. Explain that a formal way to learn information from someone else is called an interview. If possible, show children a video clip of an age-appropriate interview. Point out that the interviewer asks questions that he or she has planned ahead of time. As a class, make a list of interview questions that children could use to interview a family member about the past.

Transportation Book

 individual   30 minutes

Have children imagine that they are traveling to another state. Using the following sentence starters, have them write about what kind of transportation they might use in each time period. *In the past, I would travel by _____ . Today, I travel by _____ . In the future, I might travel by _____ .* Then have children copy their sentences onto drawing paper and illustrate each. Bind the pages into a book about transportation.

Belonging Together

 partners   30 minutes

Group together several items with something in common, such as a textbook, a Big Book, and a picture book (all types of books). Place the items on a table, and have children write a sentence telling what the things have in common. Then working with a partner, have pairs find their own group of three items and write a sentence about its common theme. Place the group around the room. Read aloud the sentences and invite volunteers to locate the group of items being described.

Then and Now

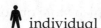 individual   30 minutes

Show children two pictures of the same location from two different time periods. Have them write sentences telling at least three ways that the place has changed. Ask children to also list at least one way that the location has remained the same.

Time Capsule

 individual   30 minutes

Tell children that a time capsule holds information about the present that can be read by people in the future. Have children write themselves a letter. Invite them to include details about their likes, dislikes, daily schedule, favorite songs, television shows, food, etc. Collect the letters, seal them in a coffee can, and place the can in a prominent location in the classroom. Tell children that you will open the can and give them their letters on the last day of school. Explain that they will use the letters to tell how much they have changed during the year.

1. **Location**   Which state touches South Carolina to the north?

2. **Location**   Which two states are directly south of Nebraska?

3. **Location**   Which two states touch Colorado to the south?

4. **Place**   Which two state names that have another state's one-word name in them?

5. **Location**   Which state or body of water touches California to the west?

6. **Location**   Sometimes part of the border of a state or country is a river. Which river is part of the border between Texas and Oklahoma?

7. **Location**   Which river is the boundary between Missouri and Illinois?

8. **Place**   Which two states have four straight lines as borders?

9. **Place**   Which city is the capital of the United States of America?

10. **Movement**   In which direction would you travel going straight from the capital of Washington to the capital of Oregon?

11. **Movement**   In which direction would you travel going from the capital of Rhode Island straight to the capital of Connecticut?

12. **Movement**   Which states would you pass though going in a straight-line west from Kansas to California?

13. **Movement**   What are the capital cities of the two states you would travel through if you went from Montana to New Mexico?

14. **Human-Environment Interactions**   In which of these state capitals would you be near a large body of water?
Helena
Sacramento
Salt Lake City

15. **Place**   Which city is the capital of the state of Ohio?

16. Human-Environment Interactions   In which city in the eastern part of the United States would you find the most people?

17. Location   Which state does Ohio mostly touch to the west?

18. Place   What is the name of a state capital named for a president of the United States?

19. Movement   The Pony Express went from Missouri to California. In which direction would a rider go if they started in Missouri?

20. Regions   On which continent would you find the country of France?

21. Regions   Which of these states is in the middle part of the United States?
Iowa
North Carolina
Nevada

22. Regions   What large mountain range is located on the east coast of the United States?

23. Movement   Over which mountain range would you travel going from Nebraska to Idaho?

24. Movement   Over which body of water would you travel to go from Michigan to Wisconsin?

25. Human-Environment Interactions   In which of these states would you be most likely to find a farmer growing corn?
Florida
Colorado
Illinois

26. Human-Environment Interactions   In which of these states would you most likely find a deep-sea fisherman living?
Arkansas
Maine
Montana

27. Place   Which state capitals have the state names in their own names?

28. Place   What is the state capital of Georgia?

29. Location   If you were in Boise, in which state's capital would you be?

30. Location   What is the state capital of California?

Why Character Counts

Respect

You show respect when you follow the Golden Rule. You can do this by treating others the way you want them to treat you.

When you respect others, you think about their feelings. You treat them kindly, even if they are different from you.

- **Trustworthiness**
- ✓**Respect**
- **Responsibility**
- **Fairness**
- **Caring**
- **Patriotism**

One way to show respect is to talk nicely to people and listen carefully to what they have to say. Shaking hands with people you meet is another way to show respect.

In Your Own Words:

How do you show respect to people in your family?

_____

_____

_____

Character Activity

Think about ways you show respect at home and at school. Choose one way and write it on the badge. Color the badge and cut it out. Wear your badge home and tell someone in your family how you show respect.

I show
respect
when

_____

_____

_____

UNIT 4 Economic Literacy

New Technology

Long ago, people made goods with their hands. It took a long time to make one good.

Technology is the tools we use to make our lives better. New technology has changed the way goods are made. Today, goods can be made with machines. Machines help people to make many more goods at one time.

New technology has also changed the way we carry goods. Faster airplanes, cars, trucks, and trains make it easier to move goods to the markets. Now you can buy the goods you want in a store close to your home.

Name _____

Try It

Write <u>long ago</u> or <u>today</u> by each picture of people working.

1. _____

2. _____

3. _____

4. _____

5. How has new technology changed the way people work?

_____

_____

_____

UNIT 4 Citizenship

Read About It The Bill of Rights protects the freedoms of Americans. It says that people have the right to belong to groups. People also have the right to live where they want and say what they want as long as it does not hurt others. Our leaders wanted everyone to know that these rights were important. That is why they put them into the Constitution.

1. What does the Bill of Rights do?

_____

_____

2. What rights do Americans have?

_____

_____

Talk About It Why do you think it was important to add the Bill of Rights to the Constitution?

Write About It The Constitution has changed little over time. Why do you think that the Constitution has changed so little? What do you think our country would be like if the rules were always changing?

_____

_____

_____

_____

_____

_____

_____

_____

_____

Native American Vest
Unit 5

Materials needed:

*Lunch-size bag

*Scissors

*Crayons or markers

*Decorations (feathers, twine)

*Tape

*White paper for booklet

*Stapler

Social Studies Skills:

*America's First People

*History

*Change

Reading Skills:

*Cause and Effect

*Sequence

*Main Idea and Details

Instructions:

1. Pop out the side pleats of the lunch-size paper bag, and press the bag down flat.

2. Trace a vest pattern onto the front of the bag. Cut the armholes from both layers of the bag.

Illustrations:

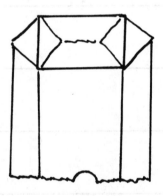

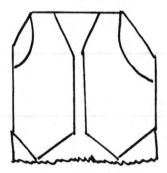

3. Cut the vest front from only the top layer of the bag. Cut a semicircle from the back of the bag at the neck.

4. Tape down the bag bottom on the back of the bag.

5. Decorate the vest with Native American designs and add twine and feathers if desired.

6. Make a booklet of the main ideas of the unit and staple it into the vest. You may also do mini-reports on the Native Americans of your area.

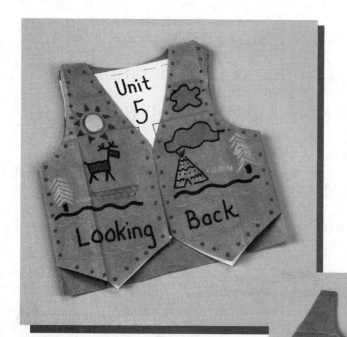

The Donkey and the Rock

An adaptation of a Tibetan folktale

Cast of Characters
- Narrator 1
- Narrator 2
- Poor Man
- Second Man
- King
- Mother
- Villagers

Narrator 1: A very long time ago, in a land far away, a poor man lived with his mother.

Poor Man: Mother, I'm going to sell this jar of cooking oil. We need money for food.

Mother: Be careful, son. That's the only oil we have left. If you lose it, we'll go hungry.

Narrator 2: The man went off to a village in the mountains.

Poor Man: This road is long and I'm tired. I'm going to sit by this rock and rest.

Narrator 1: The man put his oil on the rock and sat down to take a nap.

Narrator 2: A little while later, another man came down the mountain. He had a donkey with him.

Narrator 1: He did not see the poor man or his oil. His donkey bumped the jar and it fell on the rock and broke.

Poor Man: What have you done? You and your donkey have broken my jar of oil.

Second Man: It is not my fault the jar fell. I didn't do it. The donkey did.

Poor Man: Let's go to the king. He will us tell who should pay!

Narrator 1: Both men went to the village to find the king.

Narrator 2: The king asked them what was wrong. Each man told his side of the story.

Poor Man: This man must pay for my oil. I need the oil to sell so that I can buy food for my mother.

Second Man: I have no money. I used my money to buy this wood. The wood will heat the house of my mother.

King: I know what we will do. We will have a trial. The donkey bumped the jar, and the rock broke the jar. I will judge them.

Poor Man: You must be kidding!

Second Man: A trial for a donkey and a rock!

King: Put the donkey in jail, and someone go find the rock. Bring them both here for a trial.

Narrator 1: The donkey was put in jail.

Narrator 2: The rock was put in jail, too.

Narrator 1: It was a strange sight. News of the trial spread all around.

Narrator 2: Many people came to see. They wondered what the king would say to a donkey and a rock.

Narrator 1: The time came for the trial. The court was filled with people. The king went to sit in his chair in the court.

King: Lock the gates.

Narrator 2: The gates were locked. Then the king spoke to the people.

King: There will be no trial. You know that there is no law that allows me to judge a rock and a donkey. You have come because you are nosy. Now you must put a penny in the cup before you will be let out of the gate.

Narrator 1: The people were embarassed by how they had behaved. They gladly paid the penny and went home.

Narrator 2: The king gave the poor man the money. It paid for his oil. Everyone was happy.

The End

UNIT 5 Simulations and Games

Ways We Celebrate As a class, brainstorm a list of celebrations and traditions practiced by the children. Examples may include Thanksgiving, Christmas, Hanukkah, Kwanzaa, Fourth of July, birthday parties, Halloween activities, etc. Discuss what kinds of things children do during these celebrations. Then organize the class into small groups. Call out a celebration or tradition from the list, and have the groups act out some aspect of how it is observed. **SIMULATION**

Holidays
Christmas
Hanukkah
Thanksgiving
Fourth of July

Vocabulary Challenge On the board, write a list of appropriate vocabulary words. Also make a separate list on a piece of paper of the same vocabulary words, in random order, along with their definitions. Number that list from 1 to 10. Divide the class into two teams. Choose one team to play first. Have that team select a number. Read the corresponding definition from your list, and ask the group to choose which word belongs to the definition. If the team answers correctly, they receive a point. If they do not answer correctly, allow the other team to have a chance to answer. Provide any answers that teams are unable to identify. Continue play by having the second team choose a number. Play the game until all words have been selected. **GAME**

The Billy Goats' Route Read a version of *The Three Billy Goats Gruff*. Discuss with children the route that the billy goats traveled to get from their homes to the other side of the bridge. Organize the class into small groups. Invite each group to create a game board that shows this route. Suggest that each square on the board represent a step taken by a billy goat. Model directions to be written in the squares on the board such as: *You need a drink of water, take one step back. You had extra grass for lunch. Run three steps forward. The troll scares you. Go back to the beginning.* Provide dice and invite groups to play their games. **GAME**

Put toothpaste on your toothbrush.

Brush your teeth.

Rinse your mouth with water.

Flowchart Sequencing Select several multi-step activities with which children are familiar, such as brushing their teeth, making a bed, making a sandwich, or building a snowman. Write the steps for each activity on a square of construction paper. Choose a different color paper for each activity to make it easier for children to keep them organized. Then invite children to lay the cards out to create a flowchart for each activity. **GAME**

Act Out a Folktale Select several short folktales, such as those found in Aesop's fables. Read them aloud. Then have children work in small groups, with each group selecting one of the stories. Invite the groups to act out their story. If time allows, encourage them to make and use props where appropriate. **SIMULATION**

Find That Country Determine the country of origin for the families of children in the class. If a child's family comes from more than one country, list all that he or she desires. Make a list of the countries on the board. Then pair children with a partner. Give each pair a world map. Call out a country from the board. Have partners search their maps for the location, raising a hand when they have found it. Continue through the list, challenging children to find the locations. **GAME**

UNIT 5 Long-Term Project

CLASS PLAY: A FOLKTALE

Use this project to help children understand the cultural aspects found in a traditional folktale.

Week 1 Introduce

 class   30 minutes

Materials: folktales from around the world, chart paper

Select an appropriate folktale from around the world to adapt for a class play. Once a story has been selected, make a list of the characters, including a narrator. Discuss whether there is a need to include nonspeaking roles to play the parts of villagers, animals, etc. Then point out that a play requires other kinds of workers, too. List jobs such as making scenery, sound effects, props, costumes, posters to tell about the play, and invitations. Stress that all the jobs in the play are equally important in telling the story.

Adapt the play for the class presentation, and print scripts for each child.

Week 2 Plan and Prepare

 group   30 minutes

Materials: scripts, butcher paper, card stock, construction paper, markers, scissors

Give each child a script. Read the script aloud as children follow along. Then assign roles. Have actors and extras practice their lines and run through the play to become familiar with the words and actions they will need to know.

Next divide the remaining children into teams to perform other tasks in the play. Have children decide what the background of the play should be. Assign one small group to create a backdrop scene. Give other children the task of making paper costumes. A third group can use card stock to draw and cut out any props that might be useful. A fourth group will need to make invitations for family and other guests, and create posters to advertise the play.

Week 3   Rehearse

 group   20 minutes

Materials: costumes, props, scenery, sound effects

Give children an opportunity to complete a rehearsal of the play. Remind actors to project their voices and speak slowly. Invite some children to create appropriate sound effects for the story. Help these students find the appropriate timing for each of their sounds.

As the children rehearse the play, encourage other student groups to create the props and stage backdrops. Check for any problems with staging and props, and correct those issues before the final performance.

Week 4   Present

 class   30 minutes

Materials: video camera (optional)

Prior to presenting the play, invite children to send out their invitations and hang their posters. Help them to set up a stage in a section of the classroom or other space that will accommodate the presentation. If possible, invite an adult to videotape the play for children to view at a later date. After the presentation, discuss with children what the play tells about the country from which it came.

Tips for Combination Classrooms

 For Kindergarten students: Have children participate in the play through a nonspeaking role.

 For Grade 2 students: Invite children to assist you in the creation of the script by making a storyboard of the play that can be used to highlight the most important events.

UNIT 5 Short-Term Projects

Use these projects to help children explore cultures and traditions from around the world.

What's in a Name

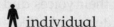 individual 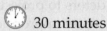 30 minutes

Materials: name origin book, construction paper, markers

Have children write their names in the center of a piece of construction paper. Then help each child look up his or her name in the book of name origins. Have them copy the meaning of their names on the paper, along with the country of its origin. Invite children to then decorate their nametags with illustrations that reflect either the meaning of their name or the country from which it comes. Display the nametags and have children share what they learned with the class.

Luz means light in Spanish.

Birthdays Around the World

 class 45 minutes

Materials: book *Birthdays Around the World*, drawing paper, art supplies

Talk with children about how they celebrate their birthdays. Then read the book *Birthdays Around the World* by Mary D. Lankford. Discuss how people celebrate their special day in other countries and cultures. Using the information from the book, create a compare and contrast chart to highlight the ways that celebrations around the world are different from the birthday parties held by children in the class. Then invite children to choose one of the cultures described in the book and draw a picture of what they imagine a child's birthday party in that country would look like. Display the pictures on a "Birthdays Around the World" bulletin board. If time allows, have children play some of the games mentioned in the book to gain a better understanding of the way different cultures have fun.

Class Tradition

Materials: chart paper

Remind children that a tradition is a special way of doing something that is passed from generation to generation. Explain that families have traditions and other groups can have traditions as well. Work with children to create a class tradition. Suggest possible ideas such as choosing a favorite class book to read together once a month, singing a favorite song every morning, or writing a class chant that can be performed before going home each day. Decide which tradition the class will begin, and with the help of the class write a description of the tradition on chart paper. Post the tradition in the classroom. Then, at the end of the school year, have children write letters to the incoming class explaining their tradition.

America's First People

 partners   30 minutes

Materials: map of the United States, research books, index cards

Assist children in finding the names of Native American tribes that live or have lived in the United States. Have children work with a partner. Invite each pair to copy the name of one tribe on an index card and one fact about their tribe. Then help them post the card on the map of the United States in the area where the tribe lives today or lived in the past. After all cards are posted, give partners the opportunity to tell what they learned about their tribes. Then invite the class to discuss the relative location of each tribe to their own community and to the other tribes.

Have children complete these writing projects to gain a better understanding of other cultures.

Class Folktale

 class 30 minutes

Remind children that many folktales were told and retold. Write a story starter on a piece of chart paper such as *Once upon a time, there was a little town with a big problem.* Then invite children, one at a time, to add a line to the story. Record their sentences as they dictate. After all the children have contributed, add an appropriate ending statement. Then have the class take turns reading the folktale aloud.

Native American Artwork

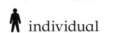 individual 30 minutes

Show children a photograph of a piece of Native American artwork such as pottery, a mask, jewelry, or tapestry. Point out the features of the artwork. Then have children write a short description of the artwork. Encourage them to include descriptive language in their writing.

Whole New World

 partner 30 minutes

As a class, discuss what it would feel like to move to a new country. Then help partners to create a two-column chart. On one side of the chart, have them list things they think might be different in the new country such as the language spoken, food eaten, or things people do for fun. On the other side, have pairs list ways the new country might be the same. Examples may include children go to school in both places or children live with their families. Have partners share their charts with the class.

Family Tradition

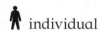 individual ⏰ 30 minutes

Have children write one tradition that has been passed down in their family. Invite them to tell when it is practiced and why it is special. Provide the following sentence starters for children to use:

One tradition my family has is_____.
We do this _____. It is special
because _____.

Chinese New Year

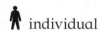 individual ⏰ 30 minutes

Discuss the Chinese New Year with children. Explain that people from the Chinese culture celebrate the holiday for 15 days beginning in late January or early February, with each day having a different special activity or event. Also tell children that Chinese people celebrate the New Year with parades of cloth dragons followed by people playing drums and gongs. Some Chinese people exchange red envelopes containing money for good luck. Stress that the holiday has added significance because everyone celebrates his or her birthday on the New Year. Have the children write a paragraph about how their family celebrates the New Year.

Going to School

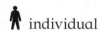 individual ⏰ 20 minutes

Remind children that a route explains how to get from one place to another. Have children write a description of the route they take to school. Invite them to include any landmarks or landforms they pass.

1. **Regions** What do you call a large community that is made up of many neighborhoods?

2. **Regions** What is a community near a large city called?

3. **Location** Which state touches Oregon to the north?

4. **Location** Which state is two states east of Mississippi?

5. **Location** Which state touches Pennsylvania to the north?

6. **Place** Which of the following is a state capital?
Denver
New York City
Philadelphia

7. **Movement** Which ocean would an immigrant from Europe cross to reach North America?

8. **Place** Which city is the capital of Massachusetts and the state's largest city?

9. **Place** Which state capital is named for a small stone?

10. **Movement** Through which state capitals would you travel going from Pennsylvania to Missouri?

11. **Movement** What are the capital cities of the states you would travel through if you went from Mississippi to South Carolina?

12. **Place** Where is the largest forest in the world?

13. **Human-Environment Interactions** Near which of these cities in the United States could you see an oil well?
Cincinnati, Ohio
Seattle, Washington
Tulsa, Oklahoma

14. **Movement** Which ocean would you cross from Africa to reach North America?

15. **Place** Which is the largest of the five Great Lakes?

16. Location   Which of these states touches the Mississippi River?
Pennsylvania
Missouri
Ohio

17. Location   Which of these pairs is made up of states that are west of the
Mississippi River?
Kentucky and Tennessee
Indiana and Illinois
Missouri and Arkansas

18. Location   Which large bodies of water are between the United States
and Canada?

19. Regions   Are the Great Lakes in the northern or southern region of the
United States?

20. Regions   On which continent would you find the country of Mexico?

21. Regions   Which states are on the west coast of the United States?

22. Movement   In which direction would an immigrant from South America go to
reach North America?

23. Movement   Over which body of water would you travel to go from California
to Hawaii?

24. Movement   What state would you pass through if you traveled north from
Arizona to Idaho?

25. Place   What are the names of the five Great Lakes? (Hint—the first letters of
the Great Lakes' names spell the word HOMES.)

26. Human-Environment Interactions   Japan and the United States trade goods. On which continent is
Japan located?

27. Location   Which of the Great Lakes is the only one completely in the
United States?

28. Place   Which state capital is named for an ocean?

29. Place   What is the name for all the people and places on Earth?

30. Human-Environment Interactions   If you lived near the Space Needle, in which state would you live?

Why Character Counts

Caring

People who care think about how they act. They think about how it makes other people feel.

You can show you care by treating other people well. You can use nice words.

You can also show you care by helping others. You can help someone who needs your help.

Trustworthiness
· Respect
· Responsibility
· Fairness
✓ Caring
· Patriotism

In Your Own Words:

What do you do to show you care?

_____

_____

_____

Name _____

Character Activity

Look in a newspaper or magazine for pictures of people who are showing they care. Choose one picture, cut it out, and paste it in the box below. Then write a sentence telling how the picture shows a caring act.

_____

_____

_____

UNIT 5 Economic Literacy

Making Choices

We buy goods we want by trading money for them.
We only have so much money. This means that we cannot
have everything we want. We must make choices. Making
a choice means picking between two things.

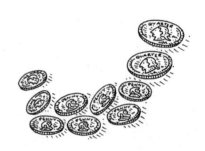

How can you decide which good to
choose? You can ask yourself which
good you would like to have more.
You might also want to think about
which good costs more money.

Name _____

# Try It

In the box, write two goods you want. If you can only have one of those goods, which would you choose? Complete the sentence by telling what you choose and why.

Choices
Goods I want:
_____
_____
My Choice
I choose the _____
because _____
_____
_____
_____

UNIT 5 Citizenship

Read About It We have many freedoms in the United States. We enjoy these freedoms as long as we follow the laws of our country. We are free to do and say what we want as long as it does not hurt others. We are also free to practice any kind of religion we want.

1. What are people free to do in the United States?

_____

_____

2. What must people do to keep these freedoms?

_____

_____

Talk About It People come from many places around the world to live in the United States. How and why does this make the United States a special place?

Name _____

Write About It We enjoy many rights and freedoms. We also have responsibilities. People must follow the laws when they do and say things. They must also follow the laws when they practice their religion. Why do you think this is important?

_____

_____

_____

_____

_____

_____

_____

_____

Career See-Through Pictures
Unit 6

Materials needed:

*Laminating materials

*Scissors

*Markers, crayons, or colored pencils

*Drawing paper

*Tape

Social Studies Skills:

*People's Jobs

*Buying and Trading

*Goods and Services

Reading Skills:

*Point of View

*Sequencing

*Main Idea and Details

Instructions:

1. On a piece of drawing paper, create a "career face" for a career you want to learn more about. Make the face the same size as your face.

2. Cut away an eye slit so you can look through the career face. Laminate the entire sheet.

Illustrations:

CUT AWAY

3. Make a list of questions you want to ask about your career. Tape your questions to the back of the face you drew.

4. Share your questions with your teacher and classmates. Ask if they have any questions to add to your list.

What's my job?

The Little Red Hen

A readers theatre play adapted from a traditional folktale

Cast of Characters

- Little Red Hen
- Dog
- Cat
- Rat
- Shopkeeper
- Miller
- Narrator
- Farmer
- Baker

Narrator: There once was a little red hen. One day she had an idea.

Little Red Hen: I want to make bread. First I need to buy seeds. Who will go with me?

Dog and Rat: That sounds like too much work.

Cat: The store is too far away.

Little Red Hen: Then I will go alone.

Narrator: So the Little Red Hen went to the store alone.

Little Red Hen: Shopkeeper, I need to buy some seeds. I want to make some bread.

Shopkeeper: I have many kinds of seeds. You need seeds that will grow wheat. Here, try these.

Narrator: The Little Red Hen took the seeds and went to find her friends.

Little Red Hen: I bought seeds at the store. Will you help me plant them?

Dog and Cat: We have plans to take a nap. We can't help today.

Rat: I don't like dirt. It makes me sneeze.

Little Red Hen: Then I will ask the farmer.

Narrator: Little Red Hen went to find the farmer.

Little Red Hen: I want to make bread, but I only have seeds. I bought them at the store.

Farmer: I will show you how to plant the seeds. First we need to put the seeds in the ground.

Narrator : So the farmer and the hen planted the seeds. Soon wheat began to grow. The farmer and hen spent many weeks caring for the plants. Then they picked the wheat.

Little Red Hen: Friends, look and see my wheat. I'm taking it to the miller to make into flour. Will you come with me?

Cat, Rat, and Dog: We are playing in the sun. We don't have time to make flour.

Narrator: So Little Red Hen went to visit the miller alone.

Miller: Hello, Hen. That is very strong-looking wheat you have.

Little Red Hen: Can you help me make bread?

Miller: My job is to grind wheat into flour. Then you must take the flour to the baker. He will help you make bread.

Narrator: The miller ground the wheat and showed Hen the way to the baker.

Baker: Hen, you have such a large bag of flour.

Little Red Hen : Will you help me turn it into bread?

Baker: I would love to. I mix flour with other things and then bake it in my oven.

Narrator: Hen watched the baker work. Then she smelled the bread beginning to bake.

Baker: Here you go, Hen. This bread looks and smells wonderful. Enjoy!

Narrator: Little Red Hen went back to the farm. Her friends could smell the bread as she came closer.

Dog: What is that wonderful smell?

Cat: It must be something special.

Rat: Hen is coming with her bread.

Dog, Cat, and Rat: We will help you eat it, Hen!

Little Red Hen: No thank you. My friends the shopkeeper, the farmer, the miller, and the baker are coming. We made the bread together. We will eat it together, too.

Narrator: And they did!

The End

UNIT 6 Simulations and Games

Neighborhood Jobs   Have children brainstorm a list of jobs done by people in their community. Write each job title on an index card. Talk about what kinds of things people do when they perform that job. Place the cards in a bowl or other container. Randomly draw a card, call out the job, and invite children to act out some aspect of it. **SIMULATION**

Occupation Bingo   Select a variety of jobs and use them to make four-by-four square Bingo cards. Be sure to order the jobs differently on each card. Write all the jobs on slips of paper. Draw out one job at a time and call it aloud. Have children match the job on their game board and mark it with a counter. As children make a Bingo, have them name off each job in their row and explain what workers who perform each job do. **GAME**

Buy and Sell   Have children work with a partner. Invite one of the pair to pretend to sell a good, and the other pretend to buy it. Encourage children to pantomime the actions involved in such a transaction, including choosing the item, handing it to the cashier, ringing up the sale, paying the cashier, and taking the item away. Have partners take turns playing each role. Then, challenge pairs to role-play similar scenarios in which a service is bought and sold. **SIMULATION**

Good or Service?   Give newspapers and magazines to children. Have them find and cut out examples of both goods and services. Then have them glue each item to an index card. Assist children in writing the name of the item at the bottom of each card. Have groups shuffle their cards and deal out five cards per player, leaving the rest in the center. Invite children to play a game of Go Fish using the cards. They will take turns asking each other for items to match those they already have in their hands. If the child asked does not have what was requested, he or she should respond, "Go find that good (or service)." The other player then draws a card from the center pile. Play continues until one player has matched all the cards in his or her hand. **GAME**

You buy lunch at the mall for $5.

Go Shopping   Brainstorm a list of ten goods and services that children might buy while shopping. Then use this list to make "Buy Cards." On a piece of construction paper, write a statement telling children to purchase the good or service for a dollar amount between $1 and $9. For example, *Buy one toy car for $4.* Post these commands on the walls around the classroom. Organize children into small groups. Give each group $100 in play money—paper strips marked $1 each will work. Bundle the strips in $10 packs for ease. Then have the groups, each beginning at a different card, shop their way around the room. Place baskets under each word card for children to deposit the correct amount of money needed to purchase the good or service. After all groups have made it once around the room, have them count their "change." Compare results to see how many groups were able to purchase their goods and services for the correct amount of money. **SIMULATION**

Assembly Line Action   Have children simulate the process of working on an assembly line. Organize the class into small groups. Ask children to prepare to do their jobs by putting on gloves or washing their hands. Give each child in the group one ingredient necessary to make a trail mix. Include items like snack-sized crackers, raisins, small chocolate candies, granola, cereal, etc. Have each child stand in a line at a table in front of an ingredient. Then begin passing snack-sized bags down the line. Have each member add a specified amount of his or her ingredient to the mix. Pass along enough bags to provide one for each group member. Give each child a bag for snacking. Discuss how making the bags might have been different if each member had to make their own trail mix. **SIMULATION**

6 Long-Term Project

CREATE A COMMERCIAL

Use this project to help children understand ways sellers try to convince buyers to buy their goods and services.

Week 1 Introduce	group	🕐 30 minutes

Materials: magazine

Ask children to describe a television commercial they have seen. Help them identify which good or service the commercial advertises. Invite children to discuss why sellers might make commercials or create advertisements. Guide them to see that because buyers can make choices with their money, sellers try to convince them to choose the goods or services the sellers supply.

Show children an appropriate example of an advertisement and discuss what product or service is being sold. Ask them to explain what they think about the advertisement and whether it would convince them to buy the product.

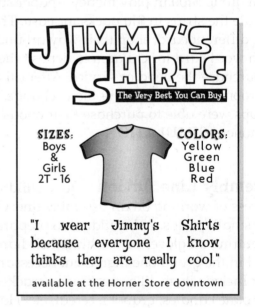

Then organize children into small groups. Give each group newspaper and magazine advertisements to look through. Explain that children will work with their group to create an advertisement for a good. Encourage groups to talk about some of the different ways advertisements make them want to buy products. Invite each group to make a list of some of the different methods used by advertisers. They can refer to the list as they plan their commercials.

Week 2 Plan and Prepare group 45 minutes

Materials: a variety of products such as cereal or a toy

Give each group a product about which they will create their commercial. Use items familiar to children such as a kind of cereal or snack food, a toy, an article of clothing (hat, tennis shoes, mittens), a sporting good, etc. Explain that groups will create a commercial to convince buyers that their product is the very best of its kind. Have children make a list of qualities or characteristics that are special about their product—what it can do best. Then have them use this information to create a short oral report, which they will use as the pitch in their commercial.

Week 3 Rehearse  group 20 minutes

Give children an opportunity to practice their commercials. Remind them to speak slowly and clearly so the audience will understand their message. An alternative would be to have children prepare poster advertisements.

Week 4 Present group  30 minutes

Materials: video camera (optional)

If possible, videotape each presentation separately. Then have children watch the tape of the commercials, much the way they would see an actual commercial. After viewing, invite children to tell what parts of the commercial would convince them to buy the good. If a video camera is not available, have children present their commercials to their classmates live.

Tips for Combination Classrooms

 For Kindergarten students: Have children tell where a person could buy the good being sold in the commercial.

 For Grade 2 students: Have them consider how buyers and sellers depend on each other.

UNIT 6 Short-Term Projects

Use these projects to help children explore cultures and traditions from around the world.

Neighborhood Streets

 group 30 minutes

Materials: butcher paper, markers, index cards, paint (optional)

Have children discuss the kinds of stores and shops they see in their town. Then ask children to work together to make a mural of a neighborhood's main street. Include buildings to represent different kinds of businesses. Help children sketch their design, and using paint or markers, have them color it. Then assist children in creating word cards to label the kinds of goods and services that are sold at each store. Post the cards in the appropriate locations.

Volunteer Time

 group 60 minutes

Remind children that people often volunteer their time to do something good for others. Help children to identify a project in their school community for which they can volunteer their time. For example, have the class work to clean up the litter or trash from the school grounds. As a class, write a letter to the school principal asking permission to do the project. Then give groups of children a trash bag and gloves. Walk with them around the school building and through the playground, picking up trash. When children have finished the project, conduct a class discussion about how volunteer work makes them feel. Also discuss the way the project helped their school community.

Pick a Meal

Materials: chart paper, markers

Work with the children to make a list of items for a healthful meal. Put this list on a piece of chart paper. Read through the list with children. Tell them they can only choose two items to order. Encourage children to choose items that give them servings from these basic food groups: fruits, vegetables, meats, dairy, and breads or pasta. Have them consider their options, then make a choice. Tally their results and record them.

Then invite small groups to use the results to create either a bar graph or a picture graph to display what their classmates would choose to eat. Have groups share their graphs. Encourage children to compare and contrast the different ways that the same information can be communicated. Pay particular attention to the different symbols used in various picture graphs.

Best Buys

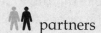 partners 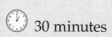 30 minutes

Materials: children's book catalogue

Tell children that they need to buy presents for a friend's birthday. Explain that they have $10 to spend. Have them work with a partner to search through a children's book catalog looking for items to purchase. Ask the pairs to make a list of the items they choose and how much they cost. When all groups have finished, conduct a discussion to compare the different purchases made by all the pairs. Find the pair that was able to purchase the most items, the one that purchased the least items, and discuss the different choices made by the groups.

Writing Projects

Have children complete these writing projects to gain a better understanding of economics.

What My Parents Do

 individual 30 minutes

Have children choose a parent or other family member to interview. Have them ask the parent what job they do and learn one fact about that job. Then invite children to write a few sentences telling about the job.

Wish Book

 individual 30 minutes

Have children think about something they wish they could have. Then invite them to draw a picture of the item. Underneath the picture, have children write a sentence using the following sentence frame: *I wish I had a* _____ _____. Bind the pages together to create a class wish book.

Where We Shop

 group 15 minutes

Talk with children about the kinds of things their family members buy. Then make a class list of stores where children shop with their families. Review the list and discuss how some stores are large while others are small. Point out that some stores sell many different kinds of items, while others sell very limited, specific things.

Dream Job

 individual   15 minutes

Ask children to write a paragraph about which job they would like to have when they become an adult and why. Encourage them to include what they will need to do to get such a job. Invite them to mention anyone they know who performs this job as a source of inspiration.

Picture Dictionary

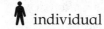 individual   30 minutes

Invite children to copy vocabulary words and their definitions onto a half sheet of paper. Then invite children to draw a picture to represent each word or concept. Have children make a cover with the words *My Dictionary* as the title. Staple the pages together, and encourage children to use the pages as a picture dictionary.

Classified Ads

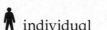 individual   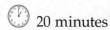 20 minutes

Show children different examples of the classified ads from the newspaper. Explain that people place these advertisements to try to sell things or to find things they want to buy. Tell the children that people also find jobs in the classified pages. Read several different examples of classified ads. Then have children write their own make-believe want ad to either sell something or advertise a job. Place the ads on a bulletin board.

6 Daily Geography

1. **Location**   Which body of water do both Alaska and Hawaii touch?

2. **Location**   Which state touches Minnesota to the north and Missouri to the south?

3. **Location**   Which state touches New York to the west and New Hampshire to the east?

4. **Location**   Which state touches both Mexico and the Pacific Ocean?

5. **Place**   Which is the state capital of Utah?
Salt Lake City
Lincoln
Des Moines

6. **Place**   Of which state is Madison the capital?

7. **Place**   Of which two neighboring states are Bismarck and Pierre the capitals?

8. **Place**   Which city is the capital of South Carolina?

9. **Place**   Which city is the capital of Arizona?

10. **Movement**   What direction would you travel if you went from Alabama to Indiana?

11. **Movement**   What states would you travel through to go from Minnesota to Washington?

12. **Place**   Of which state is Lansing the capital?

13. **Regions**   Which states border Illinois?

14. **Place**   Which state capital is the oldest capital city in the United States?

15. **Human-Environment Interactions**   In which state would you find the Golden Gate Bridge?

16. **Region**   Is Virginia in the eastern or western region of the United States?

17. **Place**   What state in the United States is a peninsula?

18. **Human-Environment Interactions**   Would a person living in Colorado most likely choose surfing or snow skiing for recreation?

19. **Human-Environment Interactions**   In which state might someone take a boat over a harbor?
Kansas
New York
Arizona

20. **Regions**   How many states border Nevada?

21. **Human-Environment Interactions**   What animal is shown on the California state flag?

22. **Human-Environment Interactions**   How many colors are shown on the United States flag?

23. **Movement**   What is the fastest kind of transportation you could use to travel from California to Hawaii?

24. **Movement**   What country would you visit if you traveled west from Alaska?

25. **Place**   Of which state is Topeka the capital?

26. **Place**   Of which state is Tallahassee the capital?

27. **Location**   Which of these pairs is made up of states that are east of the Mississippi River?
Mississippi and Alabama
Arkansas and Mississippi
Mississippi and Louisiana

28. **Place**   Of which of these states is Concord the capital?
Oregon
Vermont
New Hampshire

29. **Place**   Which city is the state capital of Wyoming?

30. **Human-Environment Interactions**   Where could you find the White House and the United States Capitol Building?

Why Character Counts

Fairness

A person who is fair treats others well. Fairness means playing by the rules. A fair person knows how to share. They make sure that

everyone gets a turn.

When you act fairly, you think before you make a choice. Being fair means you think about how your actions will make others feel. Thinking first will help you make good choices.

- **Trustworthiness**
- **Respect**
- **Responsibility**
- ✓**Fairness**
- **Caring**
- **Patriotism**

In Your Own Words:

How do you act fairly on the playground?

_____

_____

_____

Name _____

Character Activity

Think about the story of Cinderella. Was Cinderella treated fairly by her stepmother and stepsisters?

Draw a picture showing how you can treat someone else fairly. Write a sentence that explains your picture.

_____

_____

6 Economic Literacy

Saving Money

We use money to buy goods and services.
We may also save our money. We may
keep some of our money to use later. Some
people save their money by putting
it in a small container called a bank.
A bank is also the name of a building
where people can save their money.

Some goods and services
cost a lot of money. Some
people save a little money
every week. After many
weeks they have a lot of
money. Then they can buy
a good or service that costs
a lot of money.

Name _____

Try It

Look through newspaper ads and catalogs. Find pictures of goods that you would like to buy, and cut them out. Then sort the pictures into goods you would like to buy now, and goods you will need to save money to buy later. Paste them in the spend and save boxes below.

SPEND	SAVE

Write about why you made your choices.

_____

_____

_____

6 Citizenship

Read About It People in our country have the right to choose the kind of job they want to do. This is part of the law. Men and women can do the same kinds of jobs. People of any color or religion also have the right to do the jobs they choose.

To do some jobs, people need to go to special schools. Other jobs can be learned as people do them.

1. What is one right people in our country have?

_____

_____

2. How do people learn to do their jobs?

_____

_____

Talk About It Why is it important to have the right to choose a job?

Name _____

> **Write About It** Why do people have to go to school
before doing some jobs? How does school help people do
jobs? What do you think is a job that people need to go
to a special school for?

_____

_____

_____

_____

_____

_____

_____

_____

Location

Where is a place located?

What is it near?

What direction is it from another place?

Why are certain features or places located where they are?

Place

What is it like there?

What physical and human features does it have?

The Five Themes of Geography

Human-Environment Interactions

How are people's lives shaped by the place?

How has the place been shaped by people?

Regions

How is this place like other places?

What features set this place apart from other places?

Movement

How did people, products, and ideas get from one place to another?

Why do they make these movements?

Social Studies Journal

The most important thing I learned was . . .

Something that I did not understand was . . .

What surprised me the most was . . .

I would like to know more about . . .

K	What I **K**now

W	What I **W**ant to Know

L	What I **L**earned

Main Idea and Supporting Details

Supporting Detail

Supporting Detail

Main Idea

Supporting Detail

Supporting Detail

Fact and Opinion

✓	**Fact**	✗	**Opinion**
✓	**Fact**	✗	**Opinion**
✓	**Fact**	✗	**Opinion**
✓	**Fact**	✗	**Opinion**

Cause and Effect

Effect

Cause

Compare and Contrast

Information About "A"	Information About "B"

Categorize

Sequence

Event

Order

Event

Event

Event

Event

Summarize

Important Facts

SUMMARY

Important Facts

Make a Generalization

Fact

Fact

GENERALIZATION

Fact

Fact

Draw a Conclusion

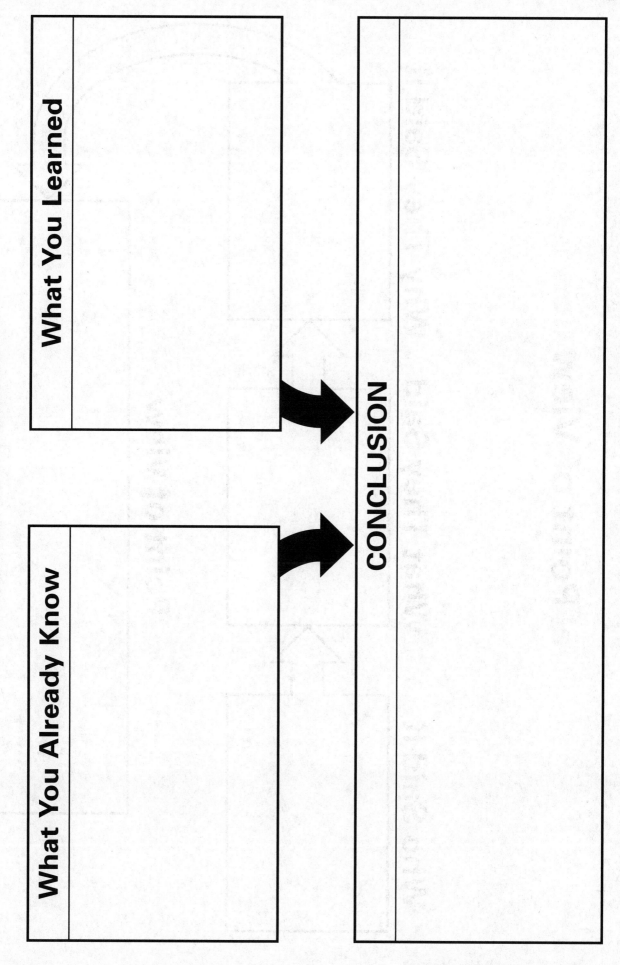

What You Learned

What You Already Know

CONCLUSION

Point of View

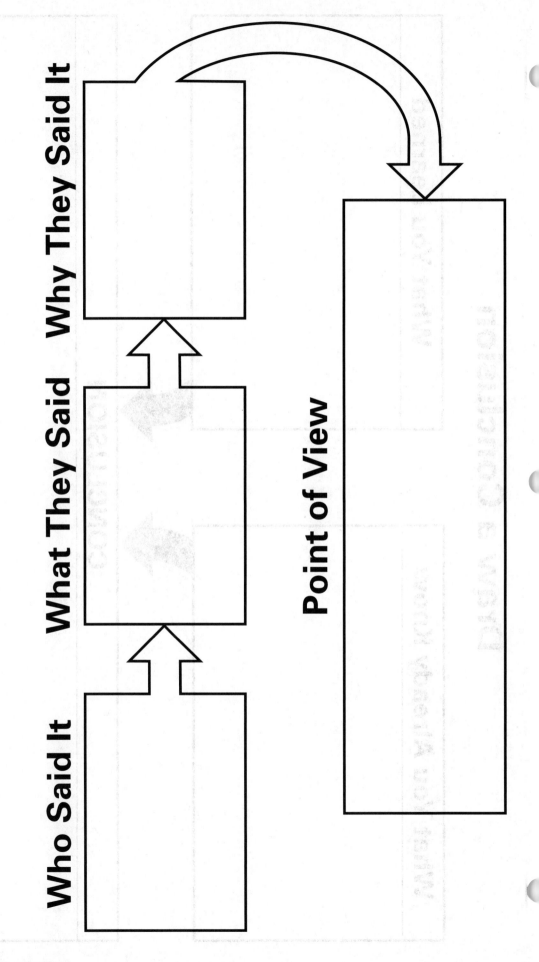

Who Said It

What They Said

Why They Said It

Point of View

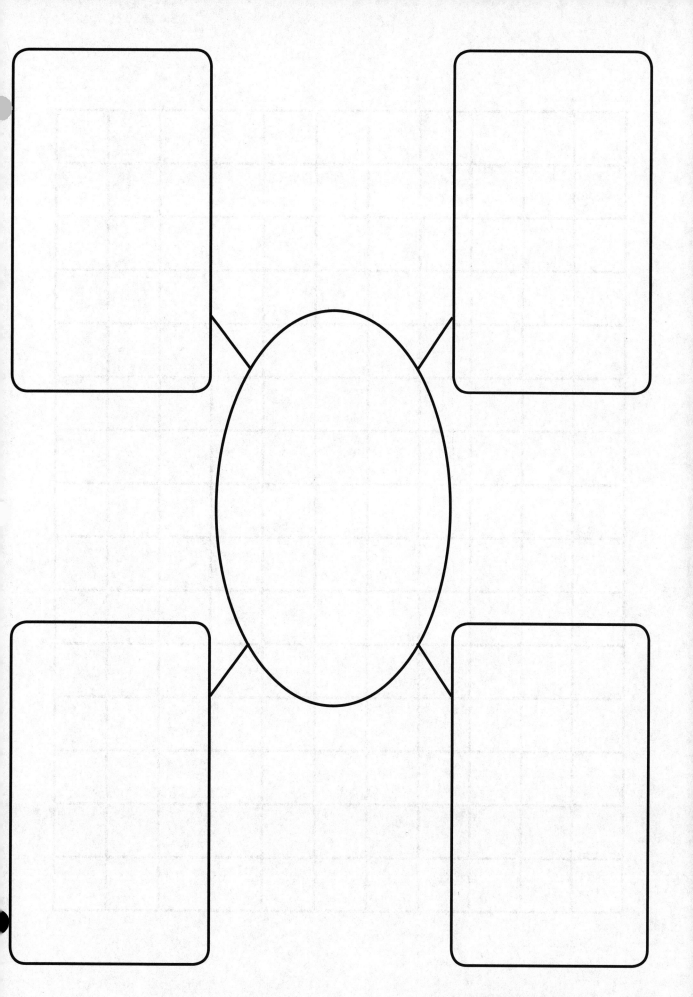

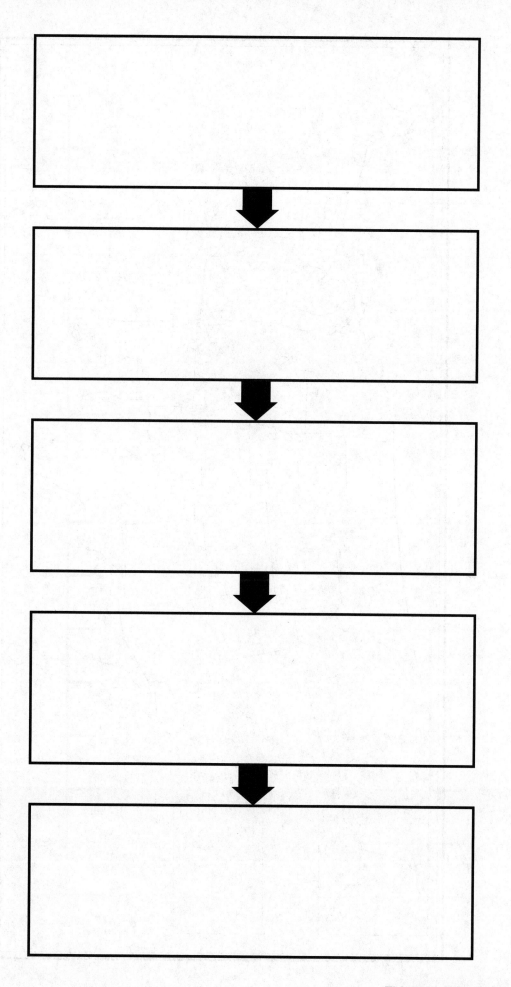

The United States

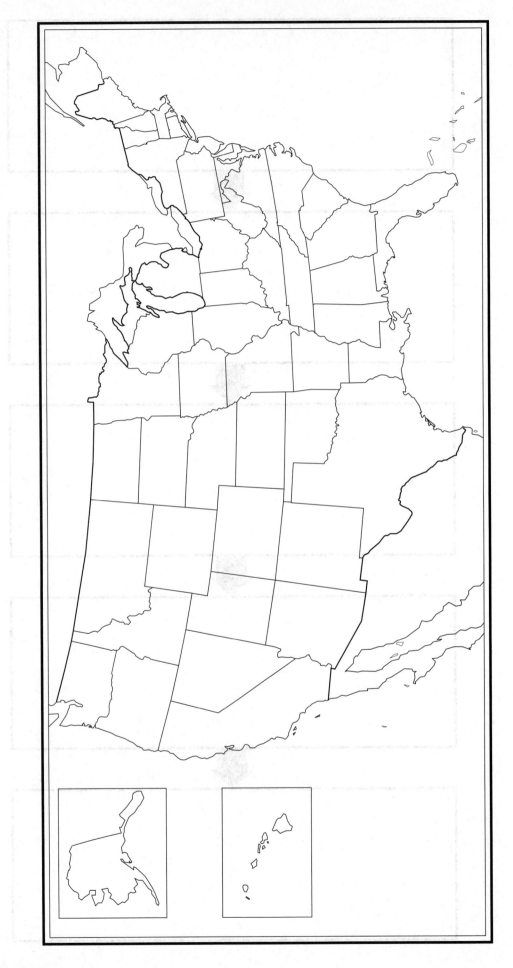

North America

The World

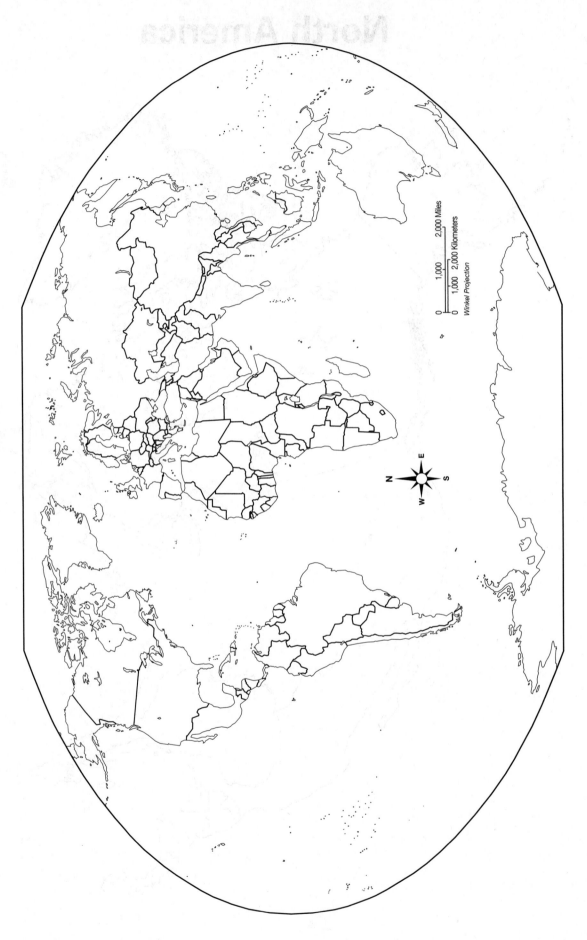

2,000 Miles

2,000 Kilometers

1,000

1,000

0

0

Winkel Projection

N
W E
S

Eastern Hemisphere

Western Hemisphere

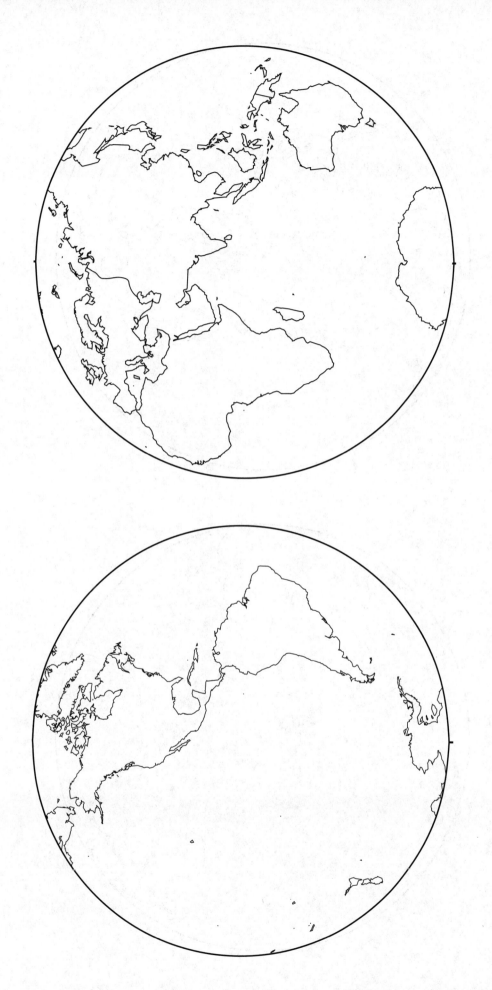

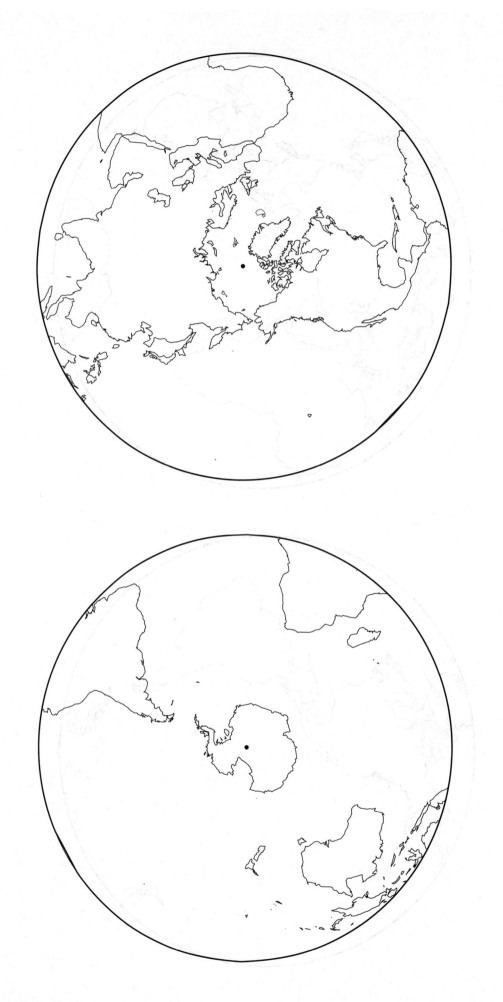

Northern Hemisphere

Southern Hemisphere

California

0   50   100 Miles

0   50   100 Kilometers

Albers Equal-Area Projection

N

W   E

S

Planning Options

♦ individual   ♦♦ partners   ♦♦♦ group/class

	Activity	Materials	🕐	Link	
Drama Activity pages 6–9	**Playing by the Rules** A readers theatre play about rules and laws.		45 min.	U1, Les. 2	♦♦♦
Simulations and Games pages 10–11	**Learning the Rules to Jacks** Children use the game of Jacks to learn about rules.	bouncing balls, jacks	30 min.	U1, Les. 1	♦♦♦
	The Mayor Says… Children play a game to learn about the job of a mayor.	hat labeled Mayor	30 min.	U1, Les. 3	♦♦♦
	Solving Problems Children role play solutions to problems.		15 min.	U1, Les. 2	♦♦♦
	Acting Golden Children demonstrate the Golden Rule.		15 min.	U1, Les. 4	♦♦
	I'm Thinking of… Children play a guessing game to review the roles of leaders and helpers.		15 min.	U1, Les. 3	♦♦♦
Long-Term Project pages 12–13	**Class Presentation: A Presidential Parade**			U1	♦♦
	Week 1 Children talk about the President's job and select a President to research.	chart paper, markers, paper, pens, poster or list of all American Presidents	30 min.		
	Week 2 Children research information about their President.	paper, pencils, resource materials, reference books, Internet web sites	45 min.		
	Week 3 Children create artwork about their President and rehearse a presidential parade.	presidential pictures, art material, posterboard	30 min.		
	Week 4 Children perform the presidential parade in front of their parents.	video camera, patriotic music	30 min.		

	Activity	Materials	🕐	Link	👥
Short-Term Projects pages 14–15	**Rules Reminders** Children create signs for school and classroom rules.	pictures of signs, poster board, markers	30 min.	U1, Les. 1	👥
	Make Ballot Boxes Children create decorated ballot boxes.	shoeboxes, construction paper, scissors, glue, markers, crayons	20 min.	U1, Les. 3	👥👥
	Comic Strip Solutions Children draw comic strips based on problem situations.	comic strips, blank four-block comic strip template, pencils, crayons	30 min.	U1, Les. 1	👤
	Classroom Chain Children create paper chains to represent rights and responsibility.	strips of construction paper in two colors, markers, stapler	15 min.	U1, Les. 1	👤
Writing Projects pages 16–17	**Elect Me** Children write speeches about why they should be mayor.	paper, pencils	30 min.	U1, Les. 3	👥👥
	Saying Thank You Children write a letter to the principal.	paper, pencils	45 min.	U1, Les. 4	👥👥
	If I Were the President Children come up with a law.	paper, pencils	15 min.	U1, Les. 3	👤
	Bumper Stickers Advice Children create a bumper sticker to promote voting.	paper, pencils	30 min.	U1, Les. 3	👤
	Responsibility Poem Children write about being responsible.	paper, pencils	30 min.	U1, Les. 1	👥
	Let Me Tell You Children write about school rules.	paper, pencils	30 min.	U1, Les. 2	👥👥
Why Character Counts pages 20–21	**Trustworthiness** Children read about trustworthiness and complete follow-up activity.	pencils	30 min.		👤
Economic Literacy pages 22–23	**Goods and Services** Children discuss goods and services and complete follow-up activity.	pencils	30 min.	U6, Les. 1	👤
Citizenship Pages 24–25	**Vote** Children read and talk about voting, and complete a writing activity.	pencils	45 min.	U1, Les. 4	👤

UNIT 2 Planning Options

👤 individual 👥 partners 👥👥 group/class

	Activity	Materials	🕐	Link	
Drama Activity pages 28–31	**Maps, Maps, Everywhere** Children learn about maps and globes.		30 min.	U2, Les. 1	👥👥
Simulations and Games pages 32–33	**School Tour** Children study routes and directions within the school.	map of the school	20 min.	U2, Les. 2	👤👤
	State Match Children learn states' names and outlines.	cards showing outlines of states and states' names	30 min.	U2, Les. 1	👥👥
	Workers in the Neighborhood Children role-play different workers.	workers' costumes	30 min.	U6, Les. 2	👥👥
	Regions Board Game Children review physical environment and weather conditions of different regions.	templates for board game, pencils, dice, counters	45 min.	U2, Les. 3	👥👥
	Sorting Challenge Children sort different objects into categories.	large sized paper, markers, index cards, stopwatch	30 min.	U2	👤👤
Long-Term Project pages 34–35	**Neighborhood Map** **Week 1** Children study how maps are drawn.	compass, maps, paper, pencils	30 min.	U2	👥👥
	Week 2 Children explore the neighborhood and make sketches of places they see.	clipboards, pencils	60 min.		
	Week 3 Children start drawing a map of the neighborhood.	local map, butcher paper, pencils, markers	60 min.		
	Week 4 Children finish the map; the map is put on display.	crayons and markers	45 min.		

	Activity	Materials	🕐	Link	
Short-Term Projects pages 36–37	**School Map Key** Children create a map legend for the school map.	copies of school map, paper, pencils, crayons, markers	30 min.	U2, Les. 2	🧍
	Design a Classroom Children design a complete map of the classroom.	blank classroom layout, stencils, pencils, crayons, markers	30 min.	U2, Les. 2	🧍🧍
	A Safe House Children discuss house building in *The Three Little Pigs* and *The Three Little Javelinas*, and create houses.	*The Three Little Pigs, The Three Little Javelinas*, recycled containers, art supplies	60 min.	U2, Les. 3	🧍🧍🧍
	What I Wear Children make diagrams of seasons and the appropriate related clothing.	copies of student photos, paper, crayons, markers	30 min.	U2, Les. 4	🧍
Writing Projects pages 38–39	**Postcard to Myself** Children write postcards.	various postcards, paper, pencils	30 min.	U2, Les. 3	🧍
	Where Would You Live? Children write about homes.	pictures of different kinds of homes	30 min.	U2, Les.3	🧍
	How Things Change Children write about seasonal change.	paper, pencils	40 min.	U2, Les. 4	🧍🧍🧍
	Transportation Book Children write about transportation.	paper, pencils	30 min.	U1, Les. 3	🧍
	From Here To There Children write about their favorite room.	paper, pencils	30 min.	U2, Les. 2	🧍
	Map Riddles Children write riddles about maps.	paper, pencils, index cards	30 min.	U2, Les. 2	🧍🧍
Why Character Counts pages 42–43	**Responsibility** Children read about responsibility and complete follow-up activity.	pencils	45 min.	U1, Les. 1	🧍
Economic Literacy pages 44–45	**Jobs** Children read about jobs and complete follow-up activity.	pencils	30 min.	U6, Les. 2	🧍
Citizenship Pages 46–47	**Property** Children read about property, and complete a writing activity.	pencils	30 min.	U2	🧍

Planning Options

♦ individual ♦♦ partners ♦♦♦ group/class

	Activity	Materials	🕐	Link	
Drama Activity pages 50–53	**Children of the Mayflower** Children learn about the children on the Mayflower.		45 min.	U3, Les. 4	♦♦♦
Simulations and Games pages 54–55	**Discussing Freedom** Children review colonists' claims for independence.		20 min.	U3, Les. 4	♦♦♦
	Date Finder Children learn important dates.	blank calendar, posterboard, index cards, counters	30 min.	U3, Les. 2	♦♦♦
	Heroic Acts Children discuss heroism and role-play a heroic act.		30 min.	U3, Les. 2	♦♦♦
	Symbol and Landmark Tic-Tac-Toe Children play Tic-Tac-Toe using American symbols and landmarks.	blank 3 x 3 square grids, pencils, counters	45 min.	U3, Les. 3	♦♦
Long-Term Project pages 56–57	**Landmark Brochure**			U3	
	Week 1 Children learn about brochures of landmarks.	chart paper	45 min.		♦♦♦
	Week 2 Children brainstorm a list of landmarks.	paper, pencils	30 min.		♦♦♦
	Week 3 Children create travel brochures for their landmarks.	drawing paper, colored pencils, markers	60 min.		♦♦
	Week 4 Children set up a visitor's center and display the brochures.	table or desks	15 min.		♦♦♦

	Activity	Materials	🕐	Link	
Short-Term Projects pages 58–59	**Class Flag** Children discuss the meaning of the American flag and create a flag of their own.	large sized drawing paper, pencils, paint, paintbrushes	45 min.	U3, Les. 1	
	Create a Holiday Children plan a holiday to honor a person or event in the school or community.	paper, pencils	30 min.	U3, Les. 2	
	Class Currency Children discuss symbols on currency and design their own money.	cardboard circles, paper strips, markers, scissors, glue	30 min.	U3, Les. 3	
	Historic Time Line Children create a time line of America's early history.	butcher paper, crayons, markers	30 min.	U3, Les. 4	
Writing Projects pages 60–61	**Hero Story** Children write about a hero.	paper, pencils	30 min.	U3, Les. 2	
	Holiday Book Children write about national holidays.	drawing paper, colored pencils	30 min.	U3, Les. 2	
	Tracking Goals Children learn to make and track goals.	pencils	30 min.	U3, Les. 1	
	Classroom Pledge Children create a classroom pledge.	large sized paper, pencils	30 min.	U3, Les. 1	
	Musical Words Children write a response to a patriotic song.	patriotic songs, paper, pencils	30 min.	U3, Les. 4	
	Settler's Diary Children imagine traveling on the *Mayflower*.	pencils	30 min.	U3, Les. 4	
Why Character Counts pages 64–65	**Patriotism** Children read about patriotism and complete follow-up activity.	pencils	45 min.	U3, Les. 1	
Economic Literacy pages 66–67	**Markets** Children read about markets and trade and complete follow-up activity.	pencils	30 min.	U6, Les. 3	
Citizenship Pages 68–69	**Declaration of Independence** Children read about the Declaration of Independence and complete a writing activity.	pencils	45 min.	U3, Les. 1	

Planning Options

♟ individual   ♟♟ partners   ♟♟♟ group/class

	Activity	Materials	🕐	Link	
Drama Activity pages 72–75	**Grandparents' Visit** Children read about the past, the present, and change.		45 min.	U4, Les. 4	♟♟♟
Simulations and Games pages 76–77	**How We Do Jobs** Children analyze the effects of technology on modern life.	paper, pencils	15 min.	U4, Les. 3	♟♟♟
	Transportation Trivia Children review past and present means of transportation and play a trivia game.	resource materials	45 min.	U4, Les. 3	♟♟♟
	Life Today and Long Ago Children compare the past and present by role-playing.	word cards	30 min.	U4, Les. 1	♟♟
	What Did I Draw? Children draw objects from the present and from the past.	index cards	30 min.	U4, Les. 1	♟♟♟
	Fact and Fiction Hunt Children sort fiction and non-fiction books.	fiction and non-fiction books, paper, pencil	15 min.	U4, Les. 3	♟♟
	Past or Present Children determine whether images are from the past or present.	various pictures, paper, pencil	15 min.	U4, Les. 1	♟♟♟
Long-Term Project pages 78–79	**Childhood Time Line** **Week 1** Children think about change.	chart paper, paper, pencil	30 min.	U4, Les. 2	♟♟♟
	Week 2 Children organize their pictures and write captions.	children's pictures, photo safe paper, magazines, newspapers, tape, index cards, markers	30 min.		
	Week 3 Children arrange their pictures in chronological order and decorate the borders.	butcher paper, mounted photographs, tape, markers	45 min.		
	Week 4 Children present the time line to their parents.		30 min.		

	Activity	Materials	🕐	Link	
Short-Term Projects pages 80–81	**One-Room Schoolhouse** Children build their own model schoolhouse.	Craft sticks, log-type building blocks, glue, cardboards	45 min.	U4, Les. 1	👥👥
	Old Fashioned Writing Children try to write using feathers and home-made ink.	berries, strainer, bowl, wooden spoon, small containers, feathers, scissors, paper	45 min.	U4, Les. 1	👥👥
	School History Children investigate the school's history and organize facts on index cards.	chart paper, pencils, index cards, artifacts	30 min.	U4, Les. 1	👥👥
	Transportation of the Future Children draw transportation of the future.	drawing paper, crayons, markers	45 min.	U4, Les. 3	👥👥
Writing Projects pages 82–83	**How We've Grown** Children write about how they have changed.	paper, pencils	30 min.	U4, Les. 2	👥👥
	Interview Questions Children create interview questions.	videotaped interview	30 min.	U4, Les. 4	👥👥
	Transportation Book Children write about how transportation has changed.	paper, pencils, drawing paper	30 min.	U4, Les. 3	👤
	Belonging Together Children write about things that are similar.	various objects	30 min.	U4, Les. 1	👥👥
	Then and Now Children write about how a place has changed.	past and present pictures	30 min.	U4, Les. 2	👤
	Time Capsule Children write letters about the present.	paper, pencils, coffee can	30 min.	U4, Les. 2	👤
Why Character Counts pages 86–87	**Respect** Children read about respect and complete follow-up activity.	pencils	40 min.	U5	👤
Economic Literacy pages 88–89	**New Technology** Children read about new technology and complete follow-up activity.	pencils	30 min.	U4, Les. 3	👤
Citizenship Pages 90–91	**The Bill of Rights** Children read about the Bill of Rights, and complete a writing activity.	pencils	45 min.	U3, Les. 4	👤

👤 individual 👥 partners 👥👤 group/class

	Activity	Materials	🕐	Link	
Drama Activity pages 94–97	**The Donkey and the Rock** Children read an adaptation of a Tibetan folktale.		45 min.	U5, Les. 4	👥👤👤
Simulations and Games pages 98–99	**Ways We Celebrate** Children act out aspects of various celebrations and traditions.		30 min.	U5, Les. 4	👥👤👤
	Vocabulary Challenge Children match vocabulary words with their meaning.	paper, pencils	30 min.	U5	👥👤
	The Billy Goats' Route Children discuss *The Three Billy Goats Gruff* and create a board game about it.	*The Three Billy Goats Gruff*, board paper, pencils, dice	30 min.	U5, Les. 3	👥👤👤
	Flow Chart Sequencing Children organize flowcharts of different everyday activities.	construction paper, colored paper, pencils	30 min.	U5, Les. 2	👥👤👤
	Act Out a Folktale Children act out folktales.	short folktales	15 min.	U5, Les. 4	👥👤👤
	Find That Country Children locate their country of origin on the map.	world maps	30 min.	U5, Les. 3	👥👤👤
Long-Term Project pages 100–101	**Class Play: A Folktale**			U5, Les. 4	👥👤👤
	Week 1 Children adapt a folktale for a class play.	folktales from around the world, chart paper	30 min.		
	Week 2 Children organize the different tasks for the play.	scripts, butcher paper, card stock, construction paper, markers, scissors	45 min.		
	Week 3 Children rehearse the play.	costumes, props, scenery, sound effects	20 min.		
	Week 4 Children present the play.	video camera (optional)	30 min.		

	Activity	Materials	🕐	Link	
Short-Term Projects pages 102–103	**What's in a Name** Children check the origin of their names and create a nametag.	name origin book, construction paper, markers	30 min.	U5, Les. 3	👤
	Birthdays Around the World Children discuss how birthdays are celebrated around the world and draw pictures about it.	*Birthdays Around the World*, drawing paper, art supplies	45 min.	U5, Les. 4	👥👤
	Class Tradition Children make up their own class tradition.	chart paper	30 min.	U5, Les. 1	👥👤
	America's First People Children research names and locations of Native American tribes.	map of the United States, research book, index cards	30 min.	U5, Les. 2	👥👤
Writing Projects pages 104–105	**Class Folktales** The class creates a folktale.	chart paper, pencils	30 min.	U5, Les. 4	👥👤
	Native American Artwork Children describe artwork.	photographs of Native American artwork	30 min.	U5, Les. 2	👤
	Whole New World Children imagine life in another country.	paper, pencils	30 min.	U 5, Les. 3	👤
	Family Tradition Children write about a family tradition.	chart paper, pencils	30 min.	U5, Les. 1	👤
	Chinese New Year Children write about celebrating the New Year.	paper, pencils	30 min.	U5, Les. 4	👥👤
	Going to School Children describe a route to school.		30 min.	U5, Les. 3	👤
Why Character Counts pages 108–109	**Caring** Children read about caring and complete follow-up activity.	pencils	30 min.		👤
Economic Literacy pages 110–111	**Making Choices** Children read about choosing products to buy and complete follow-up activity.	pencils	30 min.	U6, Les. 3	👤
Citizenship Pages 112–113	**Freedom** Children read about freedom and complete a writing activity.	pencils	45 min.	U1	👤

6 Planning Options

♦ individual ♦♦ partners ♦♦♦ group/class

	Activity	Materials	🕐	Link	
Drama Activity pages 116–119	**The Little Red Hen** Children read a traditional folktale.		45 min.	U6, Les. 3	♦♦♦
Simulations and Games pages 120–121	**Neighborhood Jobs** Children brainstorm a list of jobs and act out some aspect of them.	index cards	30 min.	U6, Les. 2	♦♦♦
	Occupation Bingo Children play Bingo with occupations instead of numbers.	four-by-four square cards, paper, pencils, counters	30 min.	U6, Les. 2	♦♦♦
	Buy and Sell Children role-play buying and selling.		30 min.	U6, Les. 1	♦♦
	Good or Service? Children play Go Fish with cards representing goods and services.	newspapers, glue, index cards, pencils	30 min.	U6, Les. 1	♦♦♦
	Go Shopping Children simulate money transactions.	construction paper, play money, baskets, index cards	45 min.	U6, Les. 3	♦♦♦
	Assembly Line Action Children simulate the process of working on an assembly line.	ingredients for a trail mix, snack-sized bags	45 min.	U6, Les. 4	♦♦♦
Long-Term Project pages 122–123	**Create a Commercial**			U6, Les. 2	♦♦♦
	Week 1 Children discuss advertising techniques.	magazine	30 min.		
	Week 2 Children create a commercial for a product.	products such as cereal or a toy	45 min.		
	Week 3 Children rehearse their commercial or prepare poster advertisements.	props	20 min.		
	Week 4 Children present their commercials.	video camera (optional)	30 min.		

	Activity	Materials	🕐	Link	
Short-Term Projects pages 124–125	**Neighborhood Streets** Children make a mural of a neighborhood's main street, including businesses.	butcher paper, markers, index cards, paint (optional)	30 min.	U6, Les. 1	👥👥
	Volunteer Time Children identify a volunteer project.		60 min.	U6, Les. 2	👥👥
	Pick a Meal Children create graphs of healthful meals.	chart paper, markers	30 min.	U6, Les. 4	👥👥
	Best Buys Children evaluate the best purchase in a book catalogue.	children's book catalogue	30 min.	U6, Les. 3	👥👥
Writing Projects pages 126–127	**What My Parents Do** Children write about jobs.	paper, pencils	30 min.	U6, Les. 2	👤
	Wish Book Children create wish books.	paper, pencils	30 min.	U6, Les. 3	👤
	Where We Shop Children write about stores.	paper, pencils	15 min.	U6, Les. 1	👥👥
	Dream Job Children write about a job they would like to have.	paper, pencils	15 min.	U6, Les. 2	👤
	Picture Dictionary Children create a picture dictionary.	dictionary, paper, pencils, staple	30 min.	U6	👤
	Classified Ads Children create a classified advertisement.	newspaper, paper, pencils, bulletin board	20 min.	U6, Les. 2	👤
Why Character Counts pages 130–131	**Fairness** Children read about fairness and complete follow-up activity.	pencils	45 min.		👤
Economic Literacy pages 132–133	**Saving Money** Children read about saving money and complete follow-up activity.	pencils	30 min.	U6, Les. 3	👤
Citizenship Pages 134–135	**Jobs** Children read about jobs and complete a writing activity.	pencils	45 min.	U6, Les. 2	👥👥

Answer Key

Unit 1

Daily Geography (pp. 18–19)
1. United States of America
2. Answers will vary.
3. continents
4. ocean
5. bumpy
6. North America
7. North America, South America, Asia, Europe, Africa, Australia, Antarctic
8. Atlantic, Pacific, Arctic, Indian
9. island
10. river
11. California
12. west
13. responses should include four of the following states: Maine, New Hampshire, Massachusetts, Rhode Island, Connecticut, New York, Delaware, Maryland, Virginia, North Carolina, South Carolina, Georgia, Florida
14. responses should include four of the following states: Alaska, Hawaii, California, Oregon, Washington
15. Gulf of Mexico
16. Iowa
17. North Carolina
18. Washington, Alaska
19. Maine
20. Texas
21. California, Arizona, New Mexico, Texas
22. Alaska, Texas
23. Rhode Island
24. Arkansas
25. Michigan
26. Oregon
27. desert
28. Alabama
29. south
30. north

Why Character Counts (p. 20)
They are honest and keep their promises.

Character Activity (p. 21)
Answers will vary. Possible answers: take care of my pet, clean up my room, help set the table.

Economic Literacy—Try It (p. 23)
1. good
2. service
3. good
4. good
5. service
6. service
7. good
8. service
9. good
10. service

Citizenship (p. 24)
1. citizens over 18
2. by voting for leaders

Write About It (p. 25)
Answers will vary, but should include three examples.

Unit 2

Daily Geography (pp. 40–41)
1. the planet we live on
2. a model of Earth
3. a drawing that shows where places are
4. what the map shows
5. symbols
6. map legend
7. north, south, east, west
8. North Pole
9. South Pole
10. south
11. plain
12. Atlantic Ocean, Pacific Ocean, Gulf of Mexico, Artic Ocean
13. Atlantic Ocean
14. Pacific Ocean
15. Hawaii
16. east
17. west
18. west
19. Florida
20. Alaska, Hawaii
21. east
22. west
23. compass rose
24. border
25. Texas and New Mexico
26. Pennsylvania and Maryland
27. Ohio River
28. Phoenix
29. Denver
30. Dallas

Why Character Counts (p. 42)
Answers will vary. Possible answers: Clean up after yourself.

Character Activity (p. 43)

Answers will vary. Possible answers: help around the house, do my school work, eat healthful food.

Economic Literacy—Try It (p. 45)

1. Mountain Town
2. Cropville
3. Coast City

Citizenship (p. 46)

1. It means paying the owner of a place for the right to live there.
2. It is the place where you live and the things you own.

Write About It (p. 47)

Answers will vary.

Unit 3

Daily Geography (pp. 62–63)

1. mountain
2. hill
3. plain
4. a country
5. Mexico
6. Canada
7. 50
8. Colorado
9. Oklahoma, New Mexico, Arkansas
10. Nebraska
11. Oklahoma, Kansas, Nebraska, South Dakota
12. Colorado, Utah, Nevada
13. valley
14. desert
15. New York
16. west
17. east
18. east
19. San Francisco
20. Australia
21. Arctic
22. Pacific
23. Olympia
24. Atlantic
25. Indian
26. Pacific
27. Nile
28. Canada
29. Pennsylvania
30. South Dakota

Why Character Counts (p. 64)

Answers will vary. Possible answers: Sing a patriotic song; celebrate the Fourth of July.

Character Activity (p. 65)

1. our country and its freedom
2. They show pride for our country.

Economic Literacy—Try It (p. 67)

Answers will vary.

Citizenship (p. 68)

1. for a better life and more freedom
2. We are free to make choices and do the things that make us happy.

Write About It (p. 69)

Answers will vary. Possible answers: don't run in school, listen to your teacher, cooperate with your classmates.

Unit 4

Daily Geography (pp. 84–85)

1. North Carolina
2. Colorado and Kansas
3. New Mexico and Oklahoma
4. Arkansas and West Virginia
5. Pacific Ocean
6. Red River
7. Mississippi River
8. Colorado and Wyoming
9. Washington, D.C.
10. south
11. west
12. Colorado, Utah, and Nevada
13. Cheyenne and Denver
14. Salt Lake City (Great Salt Lake)
15. Columbus
16. New York, New York
17. Indiana
18. One of following: Lincoln, Nebraska; Madison, Wisconsin; Jefferson City, Missouri; Jackson, Mississippi
19. west
20. Europe
21. Iowa
22. Appalachian Mountains
23. Rocky Mountains
24. Lake Michigan
25. Illinois
26. Maine
27. Indianapolis and Oklahoma City
28. Atlanta
29. Idaho
30. Sacramento

Why Character Counts (p. 86)

Answers will vary. Possible answer: You treat them with kindness. You listen and follow the Golden Rule.

Character Activity (p. 87)

Answers will vary.

Economic Literacy—Try It (p. 89)

1. long ago
2. today
3. long ago
4. today
5. People use machines that help them do the same work in less time than before.

Citizenship (p. 90)

1. protects the freedoms of Americans
2. Americans have the right to belong to groups, live where they choose, and say what they want as long as it does not hurt others.

Write About It (p. 91)

Answers will vary. Possible answer: The Constitution has changed so little because it contains fair laws. A country where the laws always changed would be confusing and unfair.

Unit 5

Daily Geography (pp. 106–107)

1. city
2. suburb
3. Washington
4. Georgia, also accept Florida
5. New York
6. Denver
7. Atlantic
8. Boston
9. Little Rock, Arkansas
10. Columbus, Ohio; Indianapolis, Indiana; and Springfield, Illinois
11. Montgomery, Alabama, and Atlanta, Georgia
12. Russia and Finland
13. Tulsa, Oklahoma
14. Atlantic
15. Lake Superior
16. Missouri
17. Missouri and Arkansas
18. Great Lakes
19. northern
20. North America
21. California, Oregon, and Washington
22. north
23. Pacific Ocean
24. Utah
25. Huron, Ontario, Michigan, Erie, and Superior
26. Asia
27. Lake Michigan
28. Atlanta (Atlantic Ocean)
29. world
30. Washington

Why Character Counts (p. 108)

Answers will vary. Possible answer: I help my little sister cross the street.

Character Activity (p. 109)

Answers will vary.

Economic Literacy—Try It (p. 111)

Answers will vary, but should contain a choice and support that choice.

Citizenship (p. 112)

1. They are free to do and say what they believe. They can also practice any kind of religion they want.
2. They must follow the laws of our country.

Write About It (p. 113)

Answers will vary. Possible answer: People need to follow the laws so that everyone will have freedom. It is also important so that no one is hurt or treated unfairly.

Unit 6

Daily Geography (pp. 128–129)

1. Pacific Ocean
2. Iowa
3. Vermont
4. California
5. Salt Lake City
6. Wisconsin
7. North Dakota and South Dakota
8. Columbia
9. Phoenix
10. north
11. Montana, North or South Dakota, Idaho
12. Michigan
13. Wisconsin, Indiana, Kentucky, Missouri, Iowa
14. Santa Fe, New Mexico
15. California
16. eastern
17. Florida
18. snow skiing
19. New York
20. five
21. bear
22. three
23. airplane
24. Russia
25. Kansas
26. Florida
27. Mississippi and Alabama
28. New Hampshire
29. Cheyenne
30. Washington, D.C.

Why Character Counts (p. 130)

Share with others and treat others well.

Character Activity (p. 131)

No, Cinderella was not treated fairly. They could have shared the work around the house instead of making Cinderella do it all. You can treat others fairly by sharing and playing by the rules.

Economic Literacy—Try It (p. 133)

Answers will vary.

Citizenship (p. 134)

1. to choose the kind of job they want to do
2. People go to special schools to learn some jobs. Other jobs can be learned while people do them.

Write About It (p. 135)

Answers will vary. Possible answer: It would not be fair if I could not do the job I wanted. I would feel bad that I wasn't allowed to make choices and I might have to do something that I would not like.